A Forlorn Hope

The Royal Dublin Fusiliers in the Kaiser's Battle

March 1918

Seán Connolly
Royal Dublin Fusiliers Association

Hell Let Loose

"Here is a man whose army history you can read at a glance: one red chevron, two blue chevrons, three wound stripes, the Mons ribbon, and the two South African ribbons. He has looked death in the face countless times. He has lived four long years in the storm of war; the red rain of battle has been his constant companion. Intense heat in the summer, intolerable flies, a thirst which seems unquenchable. Mud and slush, frost and snow in the winter: he has slept (or lain awake) under hedges, in barns, in trenches, in dug-outs. He has seen horrors about which he never speaks, he says nothing of what he has done and suffered, but deep in his eyes is the look of a man who has seen hell let loose on the once fair fields of France."

- from a description of a Great War survivor in *Forward*, the magazine of Sandes Homes, November 1918.

Contents

Published by
The Royal Dublin Fusiliers Association
Website: www.greatwar.ie

Copyright: Seán Connolly 2008

ISBN 0-9550418-2-2

This publication has received financial support
from the Commemoration Initiative Fund
administered by the Department of the Taoiseach.

Graphic Design David Lowe,
in association with the Central Remedial Clinic DTP Training Unit,
Clontarf, Dublin 3, Ireland.

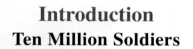

Introduction
Ten Million Soldiers

Introduction

Each one of the estimated ten million soldiers who died in the First World War represents a painful loss for family, relations, friends and comrades. With the passage of time, the ripples of sorrow have subsided and it is now impossible to comprehend the full human cost of a conflict that could have been avoided. This booklet covers the experiences of the 1st and 2nd Battalions of the Royal Dublin Fusiliers in the German Offensive of March 1918. It deals with the effect of one of the last major German offensives on the lives about 1,500 soldiers serving in a since disbanded Irish regiment of the British Army. Their experience was similar to that of most battalions faced with the colossal German assault.

Anybody starting to take an interest in the First World War will quickly learn about the famous battles on the Western Front such as the Retreat from Mons, the Marne, Verdun, the Somme, Messines and Paschendaele. While Irish soldiers participated in all of these, the major German Offensive in March 1918, which became known as the Kaiser's Battle, was particularly significant for Ireland because it marked the end of the 16th (Irish) Division. This unit had been Nationalist Ireland's response to John Redmond's call to support Britain in the War, in order to safeguard the promised Home Rule. A large number of Irish National Volunteers enlisted in 1914 but by 1918 many replacements came from England. After the Battle, it ceased to have an Irish dimension. The 36th Ulster Division also lost heavily but it retained its Irish link when it was reformed.

The German army launched its massive attack on the Western Front in an attempt to end the conflict that had continued for three and a half years. The soldiers of the 16th (Irish) and 36th (Ulster) Divisions had the misfortune to be in the frontline in the region chosen by the Germans for the main assault. The story of what happened to the Dublins during the fighting is a telling reminder of the individual human sacrifices that lie behind the mind-numbing statistics of death associated with the Western Front.

In recent years, other major battles involving Irish soldiers have received increased attention. The Irish losses in this battle that could have won the war for Germany deserve to be better known. In a wider context, the advancing German storm-troopers killed not only the soldiers of the two Irish Divisions, they also finally put an end to the idea that Irish sacrifices on the battlefield would help to achieve Home Rule in Ireland.

Despite their initial success, the Germans failed to deliver a knockout blow and the Allies began a relentless advance that recovered all of the lost ground and then drove the Germans back to where they had begun in August 1914.

When the guns eventually fell silent in November 1918, public attitudes to the British Army back in Ireland had been transformed by the 1916 Rising, the huge casualty lists, and by the earlier threat of conscription.

The sacrifices on the battlefields and the hidden suffering of the bereaved families seemed to have been of no benefit in advancing the cause of Irish self-determination. The version of history that was promoted by the new independent Irish state had no place for the men who had served in the British Army.

Ninety years on, attitudes have changed in the Republic and in Northern Ireland. The soldiers and nurses who served in the largest Irish military force ever to leave Ireland are now recognised as a significant part of Irish history. The victory at Wijtschate-Messines, shared by the 16th and 36th divisions, has, belatedly, helped to form bridges across the political divide on the island. A wider awareness of the shared losses incurred in March 1918 will reinforce those bridges and foster better understanding between the two traditions in a changing Ireland. If that happens, some good will have come from the thousands of personal tragedies that lie behind the casualty statistics for the Kaiser's Battle of March 1918.

I wish to thank Mr Tom Burke, MBE. Chairman of the Royal Dublin Fusiliers Association for his sterling work in promoting a greater awareness of a missing chapter of modern Irish history.

Seán Connolly,
Dublin,
November 2008.

Anthem for Doomed Youth

What passing-bells for these who die as cattle?
- Only the monstrous anger of the guns.
Only the stuttering rifles' rapid rattle
Can patter out their hasty orisons.

No mockeries now for them; no prayers nor bells;
Nor any voice of mourning save the choirs;
The shrill, demented choirs of wailing shells;
And bugles calling for them from sad shires.

What candles may be held to speed them all?
Not in the hands of boys, but in their eyes
Shall shine the holy glimmers of good-byes.
The pallor of girls' brows shall be their pall;
Their flowers the tenderness of patient minds,
And each slow dusk a drawing-down of blinds.

Wilfred Owen
(1893- 1918)

Chapter 1
Waiting for the Maelstrom

Waiting for the Maelstrom

On 4 February 1917, in a move that took the Allies by surprise, the Kaiser approved the withdrawal of his forces from the positions held since the end of the Battle of the Somme. They retreated to a new defensive line about 80 kilometres to the east. After the failure of the Allied Somme offensive in 1916 and the enormous loss of lives, both sides had reverted to the routine of trench warfare. Recognising that there would be no quick victory, the Germans had begun the construction of the formidable Hindenburg Line / Siegfried Stellung in September 1916 in case an allied attack north of the river Somme should succeed. The decision to retreat shortened the German front by 40 kilometres and freed 14 divisions for redeployment. They could then wait for the U-boat campaign to force the British to start peace talks.

The wary British troops advanced cautiously until they approached the heavily fortified new German positions. They had to overcome stiff German resistance to take possession of the last ridges in front of the Hindenburg Line. The villages of Epehy and Lempire-Ronssoy that were to become so familiar to the soldiers of the 16th (Irish) Division, overlooked the German line. The experienced British soldiers who had survived the costly failure of the Somme attacks could foresee that attempts to storm the new German defences would be even more difficult. The Allies now had to construct new lines of trenches and defensive positions opposite the well prepared Germans. As they retreated, the enemy had destroyed the towns, villages and railways in order to hamper the British preparations for an attack. Images of the devastated landscape were used to good effect to generate anti-German feelings. The postcard below shows the damage done by the Germans to the town of Peronne which had remained unscathed until then. It was to become one of the important bases supporting the new British frontline.

Peronne - aspect of the town entirely destroyed by the Germans before their flight.

During the winter of 1917-18, British and French soldiers worked hard to construct defensive systems opposite the new German line. They also had to repair the roads and install new supply lines, stores, hospitals and light railways as well as completing the gruesome task of burying the bodies of the British, French and German soldiers that had lain in No Mans Land since the end of the Somme offensive in 1916. The new defences were not intended to match the German underground concrete bunkers that had withstood the eight-day bombardment that preceded the Battle of the Somme. The Allies intended to maintain their attacking strategy but they had to be prepared for any German initiative. The priority was to dig good trenches and communication links and erect the necessary barbed wire barricades.

The Allies knew that a major offensive was coming. The December armistice with Russia had made it possible for Germany to transfer enough men and artillery from the Eastern Front to divide and defeat the British and French armies before they could benefit from the US forces already coming across the Atlantic. The USA had entered the war in April 1917 but was not expected to have significant forces on the Western Front until the Spring of 1918. Though a major attack was certain, the Allies could not predict where the German blow would fall. In March 1918, the Western Front was over 750 kilometres in length. The Belgian Army defended the 37 kilometres closest to the Channel. The British were responsible for the central 186 kilometres in Flanders and Picardy. The US Army held about 10 kilometres and the French were responsible for the rest. The British Commamander, Field Marshal Haig, feared a German thrust to seize the Channel ports and the cutting of his supply lines. His requests for manpower were ignored in London compelling him to leave the southern portion of his command without adequate reserves. This was the responsibility of General Gough's Fifth Army, which included the 16th (Irish) Division.

The German plan to drive a wedge between British and French armies was devised by General Erich Ludendorff (1865-1937) who had led the Germans to victory over the Russians in the Battle of Tannenberg during August 1914. He decided to aim the major attack, codenamed Michael, at the British front where it adjoined that of the French. The British defences were still incomplete, the forces thinly spread and the ground drier than in Flanders. A possible prize was the important transport hub of Amiens but a key element of Ludendorff's strategy was to use surprise and then take advantage of each opportunity opened up. A drive towards Amiens would draw reserves down from the Flanders front. Then the second phase, codenamed George, would be launched in the Hazebrouck area with the intention of breaking through to the coast. With the British disposed of, attention would then be switched to the French.

To develop detailed plans, General Oskar von Hutier was secretly brought from the Russian front. He had developed new infiltration tactics that enabled him to capture the city of Riga in the final successful attack on the Russian northern front in September 1917.

As the British were soon to discover, the approach for the big offensive would be:

- Destroy the enemy's artillery and communications on the first day in a relatively short bombardment.
- Disable the frontline line troops by gas shells to allow the attackers through.
- Define the objectives for the second day based on the outcome of the first.
- The fastest troops would set the pace. There would be no uniform advance.
- Pockets of resistance would be bypassed and dealt with later.
- Reserves would be sent to where the attack is making progress, not where it is stalled.

Colonel Georg Bruchmuller, the German artillery expert, drew up detailed plans to destroy the British defences before and during the infantry advance. A short intense bombardment would firstly destroy the artillery positions and the communication systems. Then the soldiers in the forward positions would be rendered ineffective with poison gas shells. Mustard gas was not used as this would permeate the soil and disrupt the advance of the "Stormtroopers" between the British strong-points to capture the artillery and rear positions. Any well-defended posts would be dealt with by the main infantry attack that followed.

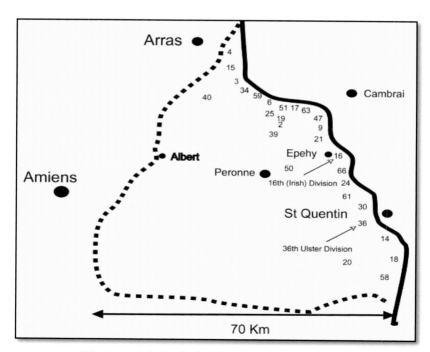

The Area of the battle from 21 March to 5 April 1918.
The location of each British division at the start is shown.

The section of the front chosen for the attack contained the 16th (Irish) and the 36th (Ulster) Divisions, two of the three divisions that were raised in Ireland in 1914 in response to the call for volunteers. The British Fifth Army under Sir Hubert Gough, an Irish cavalry veteran of the Boer War, was responsible for 67 kilometres of the front that adjoined the French Army. General Gough had twelve infantry and three cavalry divisions which were very thinly spread due to the extra allocations, in January and February 1918, of part of the front that had been held by the French. In contrast, General Byng's Third Army held 45 kilometres to the north of Gough with 14 Divisions. The line dividing the Fifth and Third armies was between Gough's 9th Division and Byng's 47th Division on the above map

The weakness of Gough's position was known but he was supposed to have the benefit of marshy ground similar to that at Passchendaele in Flanders. The weather, however, had been dry since December. There was no mud in the marshes and the River Oise was nearly dry. General Gough was informed of General von Hutier's presence and on 3 February, he decided that the main German attack would come against the Third and Fifth British Armies with Amiens as a key objective.

The Royal Dublin Fusiliers

Among the troops defending Gough's frontline were the soldiers of the 1st and 2nd Battalions of the Royal Dublin Fusiliers which were now part of the 16th (Irish) Division. They were responsible for a section of the frontline that ran to the east of the road from Epehy to Ronssoy-Lempire, The A26 Motorway was built close to the frontline in this area as shown on the map.

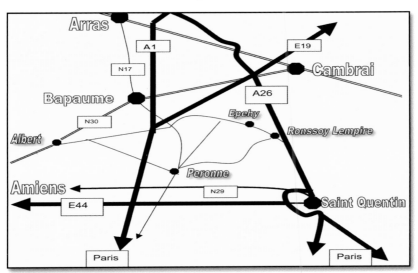

Location of Epehy and Ronssoy in relation to modern motorways.

These two battalions were part of the British Regular Army when the war broke out. The 1st Dublins had been in India since January 1910. The battalion was on its way to Flanders with the 29th Division when it was diverted to take part in the landings at Gallipoli in April 1915. It then moved to France for the opening attack of the Somme Offensive. It went on to fight at Arras and Ypres and was then transferred to the 16th (Irish) Division in October 1917. The 2nd Royal Dublin Fusiliers had gone to France in August 1914 in the 4th Division as part of the British Expeditionary Force. After the initial encounters with the Germans, the British troops had to retreat until the tide was turned at the Battle of the Marne on 5 September. At that time, the Dublins slogged for 270 km in a fighting retreat which began near Le Cateau on 26 August 1914. During that 13 day march, the battalion had passed through the area where they were now based. The battalion had also fought on the first day of the Somme before joining the 16th (Irish) Division in November 1916.

Lance Corporal C. Lynch.

One of the veteran 2nd Dublins to be wounded in the coming attack was Lance Corporal Christopher Lynch. He had been on active service since August 1914. A veteran of the Boer War, he held the Distinguished Conduct Medal, the Military Medal and the Croix de Guerre [1]

Another "Old Sweat" from the 1914 retreat was Private Bartholomew Moore, 2nd Dublins, who served from October 1912 until he was honourably discharged on medical grounds on 16 October 1918, aged 24. He never recovered from the trauma of his experience and remained a patient in what is now St. Brendans Hospital, Grangegorman until he died in 1957. Among his possessions were his treasured war medals and his Queen Mary Box [2].

Strategy for Defence

The frontline was no longer a continuous line of permanently manned trenches separated by a narrow strip of no mans land as had existed at the start of the Battle of the Somme. The strategy was now one of *Defence in Depth*, a system that had been developed by the German Army during the Allied offensives in 1916 and 1917. Both sides now had the same approach. There were number of zones, each with a specific purpose. Closest to the German frontline was the Forward or Advanced Zone consisting of a system of trenches not permanently occupied. These were supported by strong outposts, known as redoubts, positioned on the crest of the ridges containing machine guns and troops protected by barbed wire. There were observation and listening posts at regular intervals.

The Battle Zone was located on the reverse slope of the ridges. The main body of troops was located here in trenches and shelters, well protected by thick lines of barbed wire. The soldiers in the Forward Zone were to signal a German attack and to try to delay it. The main action would be in the Battle Zone. The men in the redoubts were expected to hold out for 48 hours before they could expect any relief. Further lines of defence were envisaged containing the reserves and artillery. The objective was to draw the attackers beyond the range of their fixed artillery positions into the range of the British heavy guns. The drawback was the risk that the attackers and defenders would have to fight in an area subject to artillery fire from both sides.

Further back, there was a strong and carefully sited defensive line covering Peronne and the crossings of the River Somme south of the town. About 350 bridges had been mined in anticipation of the necessity to bend the frontline back should the Germans break through. The next chapter will tell if the theory worked in practice.

Before the Attack

The Germans assembled their forces in secret by moving only at night. 500,000 soldiers in 64 divisions were now ready to attack 200,000 British soldiers in 29 infantry and 3 Cavalry divisions spread along their 80km front. The total available to Field Marshal Haig was 180,000 fewer than twelve months earlier and he could offer no more troops to General Gough. Lloyd George refused to assign additional soldiers in order to prevent their waste in another bloodbath such as Passchendaele. In the absence of an adequate reserve force, an agreement was reached with the French to come to each other's aid, if needed. Displaying a good awareness of his position, General Gough agreed on a fall back position with Haig, should the Germans break through in the south.

Von Hutier's presence on the Western Front was discovered through a letter published in a local Baden journal which was read by a British agent in Switzerland. In January, a young German airman was shot down and killed in the Fifth Army area. Von Hutier wrote a letter of sympathy to the grieving mother which he signed as the Army Commander in the St. Quentin area. The proud mother sent it to the editor of her local newspaper [3].

Gough ordered his artillery to destroy sections of the main supply roads behind the German lines. Using aerial photography, he could see that Germans very quickly repaired the damage. On 12 March, the order "Prepare for Battle" was issued followed by the order "Prepare to Man the Battle Stations" on 20 March. The order to man the Battle Stations did not reach the 16th (Irish) Division until after the bombardment had begun.

The frontline troops knew that the Germans were coming. On 20 March, the officer who completed the 1st Royal Dublin Fusiliers battalion War Diary noted:

"Enemy attack is expected any day now. It is stated now to be certain, although on many previous occasions, it was given out that it was about to take place."[4]

This is the last entry on the standard war diary form which suggests that the officer concerned had written it just before the attack began.

The view from Ireland

Despite the changing public attitudes after the 1916 Rising, the main Irish newspapers continued to give prominence to news and stories related to the war. As early as 14 January 1918, the Irish Times quoted unofficial sources to suggest "a big German effort is to be expected as soon as the weather permits". The offensive would be ""launched on the first day when the weather and the state of the ground are suitable". On 28 January, an editorial stated that the defection of Russia had put at Germany's disposal a number of new divisions estimated at anything from twenty-five to fifty. With these additional resources, the German high command hoped to deliver a crushing blow at some part of the allied line before the aid of the United States could become effective. With accurate foresight, the editorial said that if the Allies could maintain a successful defensive position during the early months of the year, "the final issue of the campaign will have been decided by the exhaustion of Germany's strength in a fruitless offensive effort".

On March 19, the same paper concluded that the Germans were ready to undertake their great offensive but were showing a great reluctance despite a whole month of fine weather. It was "very probable" that the Germans would attempt offensive action in the Balkans or on the Italian front. They were unlikely to risk their fortunes in the west until they had first exhausted the utmost possibilities of a vigorous "peace offensive". Only when that failed would the offensive happen.

It is doubtful that this edition of the Irish Times reached the Dublin Fusiliers before the latest prediction was proven to be completely wrong.

Notes

(1) Irish Times 23 March 1918.

(2) *The Blue Cap, Vol. 6, March 1999*

(3) P. Sir George Aston, in "Secret Service", 1930, p.204. He relates how General Gough came to the conclusion that the German attack would be directed at the Fifth Army

(4) War Diary of the 1st Royal Dublin Fusiliers WO95/1974

Chapter 2
Malassise Farm

Malassise Farm

Malassise Farm residence, rebuilt after the war.

On the road from Ronssoy to Epehy, two villages to the northwest of St Quentin, a signpost on the right points to the isolated buildings of Malassise Farm. Apart from the memorial cross to the 12th Division which recaptured the area in September 1918, there are no visible reminders of the carnage that took place along the British frontline that lay to the east of the road in March 1918. It was here that the 1st and 2nd Battalions of the Royal Dublin Fusiliers faced the full force of the German attack.

The farm and the surrounding area had been captured in April 1917 as the British advanced into areas vacated by the German retreat to the Hindenburg Line. Twenty-one year old Captain Geoffrey Wallace of the 7th Battalion, Worcestershire Regiment, was awarded a Bar to his Military Cross for leading forward a small party of soldiers and driving the Germans out of the farm buildings. [Sadly, he was killed on 21 August later that year in Passchendaele]. A very senior officer, Brigadier General Victor Alexander Ormsby of the General Staff, was shot by a sniper while inspecting Catelet Copse, the new frontline, on 1 May 1917. This area of the defences is now under the A26 motorway.

The 1st, 2nd, 8/9th and the 10th Battalions of the Royal Dublin Fusiliers, comprising the 48th Infantry Brigade, arrived in the area on 4th December 1917 to take over the Lempire Defences. The battalions began the routine cycle of frontline, support and reserve tours of duty. When they arrived, the weather was bitterly cold, with sleet or snow falling nearly every day. The 1st Dublins spent Christmas Day in the frontline before moving back to Villers-Foucon on 29th December, to celebrate Christmas on 1st January. The 2nd was in Divisional support at Tincourt.

When the thaw began in January, the 8/9th Dublins worked on the 18 outposts required to defend Lempire and Ronssoy. Large working parties repaired the old trenches and laid massive barbed wire fences. These two villages had been captured by the 42nd Division in April 1917 in an attack from the direction of Epehy. Unfortunately, the defeated Germans had left booby traps in the buildings, one of which exploded in the HQ of the victorious 6th Gloucesters on 18 April 1917, killing Lieut.-Col. Thomas Nott, his brother, Capt. Louis Nott, the Medical Officer, Capt. Everard Harrison, the Chaplin, Rev. Matthew Burdess, Major Robert Gerrard, and Lieut. Leonard King.

In February, due to losses and the shortage of replacements, a decision was made to disband 145 battalions and to reassign the soldiers to fill the gaps in the remainder. At the same time, the structure of a division was altered. Following the German model, the number of fighting battalions in a division was reduced from twelve to nine and the number constituting a brigade was reduced from four to three. This reduced the number of men available to a division to cover its assigned area. The amalgamated 8/9th Dublins and the 10th Dublins, which had been three of the new service battalions raised on the outbreak of the war, ceased to exist. The 1st and 2nd Dublins each got ten officers and two hundred men. The soldiers would have very little time to adjust to the new structures and battalion transfers. The inadequate assignment of troops meant that the cycle of frontline duty and reserve was postponed. Some soldiers had been on continuous frontline duty for 40 days when the attack began.

The Adjutant General issued a general instruction on 10 February 1918 to use any surplus troops to form new Entrenching Battalions which would not be under the control of Divisional Commanders. They were to be used for working on defences only and would not be deployed beyond the "Rearward Zone". The surplus of 450 men of the 10th Dublins was assigned to the new 19th Entrenching Battalion, along with 200 men from the the 7th Leinsters. The battalion was located at Saint Christ, south of Peronne where it assisted the Canadian Railway Engineers to construct the vital railway links to the front. The surplus of 497 men of the 8/9th Dublins was assigned to the 20th Entrenching Battalion along with the 3rd South Africans, the 3/4th Queens Own (Royal West Kent Regiment), the 10th King's Yorkshire Light Infantry and the 9th Leicesters. This battalion was northwest of Peronne [1].

A full battalion had about 1,100 soldiers divided into a Headquarters Section, a Machine Gun Section and four companies, each with 227 officers and men. Each company had four platoons. A platoon contained four sections of 12 soldiers. Units were seldom at full strength.

The 1st and 2nd Dublins were joined by the 2nd Munsters to form the 48th Brigade of the 16th (Irish) Division. The average fighting strength of a battalion at this time was 600[2]. As well as adjusting to the new structures, the Division had a change of Commander. Major-General William Bernard Hickie, who had led the Irish Division for over two years, became ill and was replaced by Major-General Sir Amyatt Hull on 23 February 1918.

General Hickie had been a popular leader. He had introduced special awards for bravery that became known as "Hickie Parchments" and were prized by the recipients. (One awarded to Private Ned Brierley is shown when his experience on 21 March is related in Chapter 3).

The 48th and 49th Brigades were in the frontline. The 47th Brigade was in reserve.

16th (Irish) Division March 1918

47th Brigade	1st Royal Munster Fusiliers
	2nd Leinster Regiment
	6th Connaught Rangers
48th Brigade	1st Royal Dublin Fusiliers
	2nd Royal Dublin Fusiliers
	2nd Royal Munster Fusiliers
49th Brigade	2nd Royal Irish Regiment
	7th Royal Irish Regiment (South Irish Horse)
	7/8th Royal Inniskilling Fusiliers
Pioneers	11th Royal Hampshire Regiment
Artillery	177 Field Artillery Brigade
	180 Field Artillery Brigade
	189th Army Brigade, RFA (attached)
	277th Army Brigade, RFA (attached)
Engineers	155th Field Company, RE
	156th Field Company, RE
	157th Field Compnay, RE
Machine Guns	16th Machine Gun Battalion (64 guns)

The character of the 16th (Irish) Division was now very different from that which had crossed the English Channel just before Christmas 1915. It had already suffered 20,000 casualties including over 3,000 deaths[3].

The losses and the lack of replacement recruits had led to the disbandment of:
- The 8th and 9th Dublins,
- The 8th and 9th Munsters
- The 7th and 8th Royal Irish Fusiliers
- The 6th Royal Irish Regiment
- The 7th Leinsters
- The 7th Royal Irish Regiment

The original 7th and 8th Royal Enniskilling Fusiliers had been amalgamated. Only the 6th Connaught Rangers and the 11th Hampshires remained intact. The battalions transferred in had been part of the Regular Army. The 7th South Irish Horse had been formed from the dismounted 1st and 2nd South Irish Horse in September 1917. While they were battle hardened, these battalions did not have the shared loyalty and comradeship developed during the formation, training and blooding of the Division with its particular political and religious links to Ireland. The unique nature of the 16th (Irish) Division had been dissipated before the Germans delivered the final blow in the coming days.

The Division was now responsible for 6.4 kilometres of the Front, with its HQ at nearby Tincourt. The 66th Division was on its right and the 21st Division on its left. They were part of General Congreve's VII Corps which was one of the four that formed General Sir Herbert Gough's Fifth Army. He had 15 divisions positioned immediately to the north of the French sector. To his north was the Third Army under the command of General Sir Julian Byng. Both Armies were to bear the brunt of the expected German offensive.

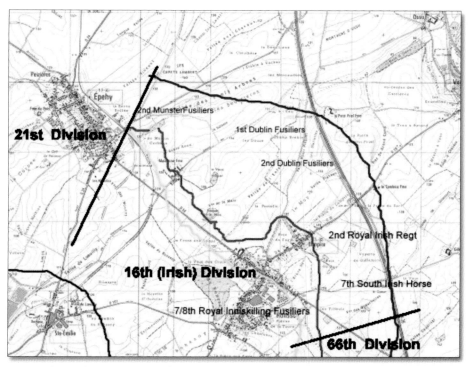

Approximate positions of the lines of defence at 4.30 am on 21 March 1918.
Based on the map in the 16th (Irish) Division War Diary [4]

The Forward or Advanced Zone (Blue Line) had a continuous line of trenches with listening outposts close to the German line. Room Trench began in front of Epehy. It led to Ockenden Trench [5], Deelish Avenue, Mule Trench, and Bird Trench. The front was well wired. Many other British battalions had completed tours of duty in the positions allocated to the Royal Dublin Fusiliers.

For example, the War Diary of the 15th Sherwood Foresters [6] has the following entries in 1917:

> *6 July: Two Companies relieved some of the (dismounted) 16th Lancers in Sunken Road and Heythorp Post.*
>
> *7 July: Remainder of Battalion moved to Cruciform Post, Catelet Post, Bird Cage, Quarries, Bird Post and Grafton Post.*
>
> *13 July: Enemy attempted to raid the Bird Cage. There was very heavy artillery fire on the Sunken Road and the Quarries. 23 casualties among Other Ranks. 1 enemy dead found on our wire.*
>
> *22 September: .....about 8.45 (am) 1 NCO was killed near St Emilie by a bomb from an aeroplane while bringing two horses up to Malassise Farm. 1 horse was also killed. Work done - revetting and improving trenches and posts.*

The frontline trenches were not continually manned as they had been in the past. Some troops would occupy them when told to man battle-stations but they could not be expected to withstand a strong German attack. The attackers coming through the first line of defence would encounter a series of strong-points positioned 200 to 600 metres to the rear. There were usually three of these in each battalion's area. They were completely wired in and could give each other covering fire. They were intended to disrupt the attacking soldiers and make them vulnerable to a counterattack.

The Germans had their outpost line along the crest of the hills in front of the Dublin Fusiliers' positions. Behind high ground, lay the German Battle Zone with belts of barbed wire in front of concrete machine-gun posts.

The 16th (Irish) Division was responsible for a 5.5 kilometre stretch of the Battle Zone (Red Line) that swung around Ronssoy-Lempire forming a definite salient. This was where the main body of the 16th (Irish) Division's infantry was intended to stop the attack head on. The meandering Ridge Reserve trench followed the contours along the ridge to the north east of the Epehy/Ronssoy road. The village of Ronssoy-Lempire was turned into a fortress surrounded by trenches and barbed wire defences.

There were very few dugouts in the layout. The long communication trenches such as Deelesh Avenue and St Patrick's Avenue, enabled the soldiers to move safely to the frontline and back. There were a number of tall concrete observation towers for the artillery, two of which can still be seen in Epehy [7].

The valley to the northeast of May Copse was shown on the Trench Map as "St Patrick's Valley". It is now shown on maps as Vallee de l'Enfer (Valley of Hell).

The third line of defence (Yellow Line) ran along the other side of the Epehy/Ronssoy road and in front of Ronssoy Wood. This is where the reserve troops were to be stationed. Further back were two more defensive lines. The Brown Line was in front of St Emilie and the Green Line was in front of Tincourt and Hamel. Barbed wire defences had been built but the Green Line had yet to be dug.

The 48th Brigade was responsible for the front between Epehy and Ronssoy/Lempire. Its three battalions each had two companies in the Forward Zone and two in the Battle Zone. The details given in the Defence Scheme for the 1st Battalion [(8)] show how the *Defence in Depth* strategy created enormous risks for the companies unfortunate enough to be on duty in the frontline when the massive German attack came. The best that they could hope to achieve would be to delay the advancing troops while preparations were made for a major action in the Battle Zone. There were no plans for their evacuation.

During the first two weeks of March, a number of raids on the German positions had been organised. The British commanders wanted information on the new German divisions that were rumoured to be moving up. During the winter months, these had been taken away from the front for training in the new methods of attack. They were assembled at the big railway junctions such as Valenciennes, Maubeuge, Wassigney and Vervins and then marched on seven successive nights to reach their starting positions the night before the attack.

On the 15th March, Corporal Robert George Spratt died of wounds and is buried in the nearby cemetery at Villers-Faucon. He had worked in the Land Commission in Merrion Street, Dublin. His name is on the memorial which was erected in the entrance hall of the Commission. This was left in place when the Merrion Hotel converted the building. Corporal Spratt had originally joined the Black Watch, the Royal Highland Regiment, like some of his former colleagues also commemorated on the memorial.

Prisoners captured by the 2nd Royal Munster Fusiliers on the following night confirmed the rumours of the new German units in the area. At 3 a.m. on St Patrick's Day, Captain Kee led a sixty strong group in a raid on Kildare Post to try to identify the new German divisions but nobody was found. Inaccurate shooting by the British Artillery killed one of their own soldiers and wounded five others. Private William Edward Robbins, aged 19, from Almonsbury Hill, Bristol, died from wounds on this day. He had been reassigned from the Training Reserve. He was also buried in Villers-Faucon Communal Cemetery Extension.

Land Commission Memorial, Merrion Hotel, Dublin.

On the night of 19 March, there were two more raids. Lieutenants Addis and Quigley led thirty soldiers from the 2nd Dublins into the German trenches north of Lark Post and killed six Germans, wounded several more, and brought back a wounded prisoner through Mule and Heythrop trenches. Lance Corporal Thomas Byrne from Dublin was killed in the raid. He has no known grave.

Lieutenant Williamson led a smaller group of ten 1st Dublins into the German lines at Holts Bank at 3 a.m. but did not encounter anyone. They remained in the enemy position until dawn and returned safely.

The Plan for Defence

A formal report on the operations of the 16th (Irish) Division in the period from 21-25 March was prepared on 29 April. This contained a detailed map of the disposition of the 1st and 2nd Dublins at 4.30 a.m. on 21 March. It shows that most of the troops were in the Battle Zone. This diagram probably represents the positions to be taken when ordered to "Man Battle Stations". This command was not issued to the 16th Division until 5 a.m. on the day of the attack and was forwarded to the brigades 20 minutes later.

Disposition at 4.30 a.m. on 21 March 1918 WO 95/1956

The above map shows the precarious position companies assigned to the Forward Zone. In the event of a major attack, the thinly spread groups near the frontline would be quickly surrounded and would have no opportunity to escape. There were few communication trenches leading to the rear.

Positions held by the 1st Battalion, Royal Dublin Fusiliers

The battalion War Diaries contain more precise information about the positions of the companies. The battalion was holding the central sub-section of the 48th Brigade front. It had 28 Officers and 645 other ranks to hold a front of about 1,500 metres from the east edge of Malassise Farm to May Copse inclusive.

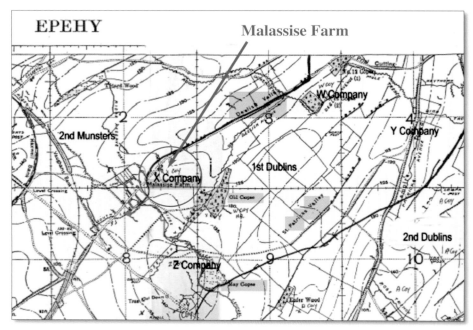

It had two companies in the Forward Zone and two in the Battle Zone. "Y" Company, under Acting Captain H. M. Letchworth, was allocated the right front position. Lieutenant Williamson had led the small raid from this company on 19 March. The A26 motorway now runs through what would have been No Mans Land in front of this position. There were three platoons in the frontline trench opposite Petit Priel Farm. (This farm was re-built after the war and can be reached by taking the road under the motorway and going up the hill to the right).The fourth platoon was in shelters to their rear along Lempire Road in readiness for a counter attack. The company HQ was at a position known as "The Nest". The map coordinates locate this, appropriately enough, at the junction of Bird Trench, Mule Trench and St Patrick's Avenue Trench (where the number 4 for that quadrant is shown on the map). Even after ninety years, the positions of some of these trenches can be seen when the land has been ploughed as there is still a different soil colouration where the soil had been disturbed. One of the Sergeants in this company was Francis Lyons, the son of John Lyons, 17 Werburgh St., Dublin. He was killed on the opening day of the attack.

"W" Company, under Second-Lieutenant Cox, was at the left front position. It had two platoons in Mule Trench. The Company HQ and a reserve platoon were in Old Copse wood to the east of Malassie Farm. The fourth platoon was southwest of No. 12 Copse. These wooded landmarks survived the destruction and are useful for orientation.

The platoons in the frontline trenches were about 2km from the Ridge Reserve Trench which was part of the Red Line.

"Z" Company was in Right Support with the Company HQ and two platoons in St. Patrick's Valley. The other two platoons were in the Central Reserve Trench, the Red Line, in the vicinity of May Copse.

"X" Company was in Left Support with the Company HQ and two platoons in Malassise Farm. One platoon was in shelters in Old Copse. The other platoon was in a strongpoint across the road that runs north from the farm. Captain Kee and Second-Lieutenant Thompson had led the fruitless raid from this company on St. Patrick's Day.

The Battalion HQ was in "the old battery position about 200 yards in the rear of the centre". Major John P. Hunt was in command.

In the case of an attack, the instructions were to hold the frontline "at all costs". The two support companies were to "man the Red Line and hold on to the last." Should Epehy or Malassise Farm be taken, the battalion was to form a defensive flank against the Germans trying to turn the flank through Lempire.

Positions held by the 2nd Battalion, Royal Dublin Fusiliers

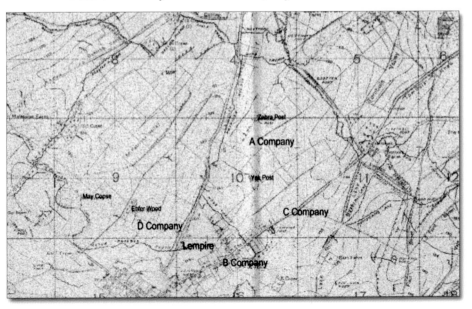

The 2nd Dublins held the line from May Copse to Lempire West. They had 23 Officers and 643 Other Ranks. Major Wheeler was in command, Captain Byrne was second in command, Captain Stitt was the adjutant and Rev. Fr Casey was the chaplain. They had been in the trenches for 40 days.

"A" Company, under the command of Captain Cunningham, was the left front company. Second-Lieutenant O'Connell was in charge of a platoon in Zebra post. Second-Lieutenant Jackson's platoon was in Yak Post. The Company HQ was in Rose Trench with Second-Lieutenant Addis' two platoons.

"C" Company under Captain Karney and Second Lieutenants Petit and Wilkin, was the right front company. It had three platoons in Sandbag Alley and part of Ridge Reserve South, with the Company HQ and one platoon in Ronssoy.

"D" Company, under Capt Addis, had one platoon in Enfer Wood, an isolated post in front of the Red Line, two platoons in Ridge Reserve and one platoon to the rear in Quid Trench.

"B" Company under Captain Lawrence, Lieutenant Lloyd and Second-Lieutenant Quigley, was in support in Ridge Support.

The 2nd Dublins' HQ was in Ronssoy but it was moved up to Ridge Support when the battle began. Lieutenants Addis and Quigley had led the successful raid on the German trenches on the night on 19 March.

The Other Irish Units

The third battalion of the 48th Brigade was the 2nd Munsters. They were responsible for the area to the left, between Tetard Wood and Malassise Farm. They had 22 Officers and 629 Other Ranks. They had been in the frontline since 22 February.

The 49th Brigade held the positions to the right. Most of the men of this and the 48th Brigade were in the advance Zone because of the fear of a surprise attack. Major-General Hull wanted to have one brigade in the Advance zone and one in the Red Zone but he was overruled by Generals Congreve and Gough.

Further south, in front of St. Quentin, the men of the 36th (Ulster) Division were also expecting the German attack and were to suffer a fate similar to that of the 16th (Irish) Division.

Notes

(1) http://www.1914-1918.net/entrenching.htm

(2) Johnstone, p.340

(3) Denman, p.128

(4) National Archives, London WO95/1956

(5) Sergeant James Ockenden, 1st RDF, was awarded the Victoria Cross for Gallantry on 4 October 1917 near Langemarck in Belgium.

(6) WO95/2488

(7) The observation tower at Cullen post is in a garden on the left of the road signposted to Pigeon Ravine Cemetery where the D58 from Ronssoy enters Epehy. There is a second tower at Morgan's Post at the northern end of the village at the junction of the D58 with the D24 road to Villers-Guislain

Petit Priel Farm, rebuilt after the war.

During the retreat in August 1914, four British soldiers became isolated from their regiments. They were befriended by some residents of the nearby village of Villeret who hid them from the Germans for nearly two years. Privates Thomas Donoghue and David Martin were with the 1st Royal Irish Fusiliers. Their comrades in hiding were Privates Robert Digby, 1st Hampshires and William Thorpe, 1st King's Own (Royal Lancaster Regiment). They were eventually betrayed in May 1916 and executed by the Germans. They are buried in the churchyard of nearby Le Catelet. David Martin was the husband of Mary Martin of 2 Athens Street, Woodstock Road, Belfast. Robert Digby had a relationship with the local girl Claire Dessene and they had a daughter who was named Helene. The story is told in "The Englishman's Daughter: A True Story of Love and Betrayal in World War I" by Ben Macintyre, published by Random House, 2001.

Waiting in the Trenches.

Chapter 3
The Downpour of Death

The Downpour of Death: March 21, 1918

At 4.40 a.m., on 21 March, 1918, over 6,000 pieces of German artillery began a five-hour bombardment of the British Third and Fifth Armies along an 80 kilometre front. Over 1,160,000 shells were fired, including gas and high explosives in accordance with a precise timetable. The main initial targets were the British positions in the Battle Zone (the Red Line), the communication systems and the artillery in Ste. Emilie and Villers-Foucon. Towards the end of the bombardment, the target was switched to the frontline positions containing the forward troops. These were drenched with poison gas shells which made the soldiers incapable of dealing with the attackers. The layout of the British defences was precisely known to the German planners as German planes had made many reconnaissance flights over the British lines in the preceding weeks. The telephone lines were cut and communication was impossible

As the dawn broke, the countryside was shrouded in a thick mist that reduced visibility to about twenty-five metres. The British soldiers unlucky to be in the frontline at this time could not see if or when the Germans were advancing. The British machine gunners, so carefully positioned to cut down any German soldiers breaking through the frontline, could not see through the mist. In contrast, the lack of visible targets did not prevent the German gunners directing their shells at predetermined British positions where the soldiers were sheltering.

The anxious soldiers had to endure the shelling in poorly protected positions while wearing their gas masks. Few of the survivors ever spoke about the experience but some idea of the horror can be glimpsed in the German veteran Ernst Junger's description of how it felt to be on the receiving end of such a bombardment in his classic "Storm of Steel":

> *"You must imagine you are securely tied to a post, being menaced by a man swinging a heavy hammer. Now the hammer has been taken back over his head, ready to be swung, now it's cleaving the air towards you, on the point of touching your skull, then it's struck the post, and the splinters are flying – that's what it's like to experience heavy shelling in an exposed position"* [1]

At 9.30 a.m. a further 3,500 mortars shelled the forward British defences in a final crescendo. Five minutes later, 60 divisions containing 500,000 German soldiers began to advance through the mist. Forty divisions attacked the 67 kilometres of the front held by Gough's Army. Sir Arthur Conan Doyle was of the opinion that "never in the history of the world had a more formidable force been concentrated upon a fixed and limited objective" [2]. The relative shortness of the bombardment would also have contributed to the surprise. Previous large British attacks on the German lines had been preceded by days of shelling to ensure that all defences were destroyed. Germans now appeared out of the mist before the British soldiers expected them.

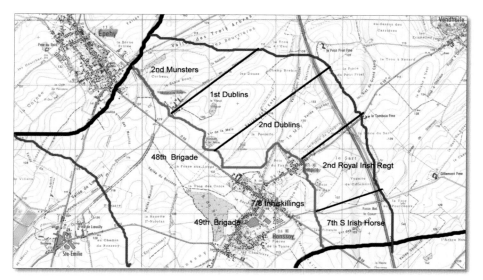

Approximate positions of 16th Division at 4.40 a.m. on 21 March

The 48th Brigade containing the 1st and 2nd Dublins and the 2nd Munsters were at the left of the 16th Irish Division's position. During the day, they managed to withstand the direct attack on their positions but the Germans managed to made an early break-through at the junction with the 66th Division at the side of the salient. They surrounded the Ronssoy/Lempire defences, attacked the Dublins from their right along the main trenches and threatened to come behind them. The 2nd Royal Irish Regiment held out until 1.30 p.m. but their Commanding Officer. Lt. Col. Scott was killed. Only 1 Officer and about 40 other ranks of the 7th South Irish Horse managed to withdraw. They reached Ste. Emilie at about 7 p.m.

By midnight, the 47th Brigade was holding the Brown Line while the remnants of the 48th and 49th moved further back to Villers Faucon..

In the confusion, the 6th Connaught Rangers had been ordered to move up to Ronssoy Wood with two tanks to make a counter-attack in accordance with the defence plan. The attack was launched in the afternoon without any artillery support and was repelled with heavy losses. The CO of the 49th Brigade had cancelled the operation but was unable to contact the battalion in time.

The 1st Battalion, Royal Dublin Fusiliers

The War Diary for the 1st Dublins for the period 21–31 March was not written on the standard form and it appears to have been completed at the end of the retreat. The detailed entries for the first day of the attack describe how the inadequate defences were overwhelmed by the German advance from the front and flank:

4.45 am: An intense barrage with gas shells was opened by enemy all along front and battery positions. Visibility was rendered impossible by a very thick mist. Our batteries at once replied but were speedily neutralised, presumably by the effects of gas. Few casualties from gas occurred among the troops holding the line owing to the prompt adjustment of Box Respirators.

8.45 am: As far as can be judged, the gas barrage gave way to HE (High Explosive) at about 8.45 am.

10.45 am: The HE barrage continued 'til 10.45 a.m. and by this time the gas had sufficiently cleared to allow the removal of Box Respirators.
At 10.45 am "Z" Coy on the left reported the enemy attacking the Red line.

10.55 am: At 10.55 am "W" Coy in centre reported that enemy had entered the Red line in the vicinity of May Copse but had been ejected.

11.10 am: At about 11.10 am. "Y" Coy on right reported that the 2nd Battalion Royal Dublin Fusiliers had withdrawn and that the Right flank was exposed. "X" Coy in support sent two platoons to reinforce Right flank: remaining two platoons reinforced "Y" Coy which had up to now suffered severely from casualties.

11.50 am: The Centre was again heavily attacked at 11.50 a.m. and compelled to fall back on support line, in consequence the enemy effected a footing on the Lempire-Epéhy Road.

11.55 am: At about 11.50 am the mist cleared slightly and it was possible to form some idea of the situation – on the left the 2nd Battalion R. Munster Fusiliers still held the Red line. On the Right, touch had been lost with the 2nd Batt R. Dublin Fusiliers who had been withdrawn and further to the Right, the Right Brigade could be seen withdrawing through Ronssoy.

12 Noon: About 12 Noon, Brigade HQ was informed of the situation by telephone as far as it was known and it was agreed that the Battalion should hold its ground and, if forced, to withdraw to make a defensive flank for the 2nd R. Munster Fusiliers.

12.20 pm: At About 12.20 pm, the enemy were seen to be advancing through Ronssoy and our artillery were seen being withdrawn.

12.40 pm: At 12.40 pm one of our tanks was observed proceeding to counter attack up the St Emilie- Ronssoy Road.

12.50 pm: At 12.50 pm reports from wounded showed that the troops in the Red line were very hard pressed and about this time a message was received from O.C. "Y" Coy on the Right reporting his position surrounded and that he would hold out to the end. (O.C. "Y" Coy A/Capt H.M. Letchworth) The personnel of Battalion HQ now manned the Sunken Road at Battalion HQ, ready to defend the Right flank.

1.50 pm: The remnants of the RED line held out until overwhelmed about 1.50 pm when the enemy were observed all along the camouflage along the Epéhy-Lempire Road.

The position of Battalion HQ was being swept by M.G. fire at close range and enemy were seen to be working around the right flank from Ronssoy Wood.

2.05 pm: At about 2.05 pm telephone communication with Bde HQ which had been cut, was restored and the situation discussed. It was agreed that the remnants of the Battalion should withdraw to the Railway Embankment just South East of St Emilie-Malassise Road and protect the Right Flank of the 2nd Munster Fusiliers.

2.30 pm: This withdrawal was effected by the Battalion, now 70 strong in pairs by 2.30 pm and a position established to command the Lempire-Epéhy Road.

2.45 pm: About 2.45 pm, about 30 men had been collected in the Brown Line immediately East of the Quarry. These were mostly stragglers collected by NCOs.

3.15 pm: The party on the Railway Embankment effected touch with a battalion of the Leicester Regiment (39 Division) who had moved up in support of the 2nd Royal Munster Fusiliers.

4.15 pm: At 4.15 pm Enemy opened intense barrage on Brown Line attacking S.E. of St Emilie.

5.30 pm: At about 5.30 pm, the party on the Railway had their right flank turned and, finding it impossible to further hold their position, fell back in good order through the Leicestershire Regiment to the Brown Line which was reached at 6 pm and joined up with the details of the Battalion holding it. It is estimated that the enemy lost heavily in his assault on the Red Line and particularly heavy in front of our position on the Railway – about 80 or 90 were killed in the old Battery position which had been Battalion HQ.

8.45 pm: The 47th Brigade having taken over the Brown Line, the Battalion was withdrawn and, reinforced with details from Transport lines, took up a position from the Quarry to the Sugar Factory at St Emilie effecting touch with the 11th Hants on the Right.

Midnight: At 12 midnight, the Battalion withdrew to Divisional HQ (Tincourt) to reorganise, arriving there about 4 am. [3].

When the battalion withdrew at 2.30 p.m., it was missing over 600 soldiers. When the official records were compiled after the war, the deaths of 45 of them were officially recorded for 21 March. This was the lowest number for the Division. Others who were killed on this day may have been assigned to a later date due to the lack of precise information. Almost 75% have no known grave and their names are on engraved on the Pozieres Memorial.

The 2nd Dublins and the other battalions to the right bore the brunt of the German breakthrough into the salient.

The Second Battalion, Royal Dublin Fusiliers

Second Lieut. Christopher Quigley,
4 St. John's Gardens
Islandbridge Dublin.

The War Diary for the 2nd Battalion is also written on plain paper but is less detailed. It states that the Germans attacked along the whole front at 11.15 a.m. The mist prevented any observation. All companies were in their battle positions when the Germans reached Sandbag Alley where they were held up by the companies in the Red Line.
 The Diary states:

"2/Lieut. G. Quigley and a Party of 20 Other Ranks pushed forward in front of the Red Line to deal with an enemy Machine Gun which had worked close up to our line. The gun and team were destroyed. When the party were returning 2/Lieutenant Quigley was killed".

At about 12.30 p.m. the troops on our right flank which were holding Lempire East Defences were seen to be withdrawing. This exposed our right flank. Shortly afterwards the enemy appeared in the villages of Lempire and Ronssoy and brought enfilade fire on our position. "A" and "C" Companies were isolated. Our position then became untenable and withdrawal to the Brown Line was commenced from the Left. This was carried out in good order, supported by Rifle and Lewis Gun fire".

The Battalion occupied the Brown Line about 3 p.m. where it remained in position until relieved by the 47th Infantry Brigade at about 4 a.m. on the 22nd March, 1918." (4)

The withdrawal was covered by two Lewis machine-gunners who took up one position after the other to delay the German pursuit. The initial group that reached the Brown Line consisted of seven officers and two hundred NCOs and men. They were joined by some stragglers from their own and other battalions. These were organised into platoons to help repel any German attack. Shortly after 3 p.m. the Germans opened fire on the Brown Line with heavy artillery. The shelling continued until after dusk. The Germans launched an infantry attack around 6 p.m. that was driven back.

The 6th Connaught Rangers relieved the battalion and it spent the few hours before dawn in the Railway Cutting to the west of the village of St Emile. This was about 3.5km from the frontline.

The records show that 117 had been killed in action on this day. Almost 80% have no known grave, their names being engraved on the Pozieres Memorial. The higher number of deaths in this battalion may have been caused by the fact that German assault came from their flank and not from the front as anticipated. Their resistance gave more time to the 1st Dublins to withdraw before they were surrounded.

The 19th and 20th Entrenching Battalions

In the afternoon, the Dublin Fusiliers in the 19th Entrenching Battalion were ordered to prepare to move and later in the evening they travelled by lorry to Vraignes-en-Vermandois along the already congested roads. The 20th remained working on the light railway.

Malassise Farm.

The 2nd Munsters were responsible for the Ridge Reserve North Trench (the Red Line) between Tetard Wood and Malassise Farm. "D" Company and some of "B" and "C" Companies of the battalion were here. About 200 metres in front, two platoons were located in two strong points in Room Trench which was otherwise unmanned. When the mist began to clear about 11 a.m., Lt-Col Ireland went forward to assess the situation and was mortally wounded. The Munsters inflicted severe casualties on the troops assembled opposite in Catelet Valley. They prevented the enemy moving artillery up the Malassise Road until after 4 p.m. by shooting the drivers and horses. When the Germans succeeded in taking the positions of the Dublins on their right flank, the garrison in Malassise Farm was open to an attack from three sides. An attack was launched from Old Copse, which was successful despite the tough defence led by Lieutenant P. L. Cahill, who had moved up from the reserve position. The enemy now continued the attack along Ridge Reserve North Trench using trench mortars. The fight lasted until 5 p.m., when some of the Munsters managed to withdraw under the cover of darkness[(5)]. A group under Lieutenants Whelan and Denahy, managed to hold out in Epehy until noon the next day, when they had "fired their last round and thrown their last bomb before surrendering" [(6)]. Lieutenant H.H.Whelan, M C, who was from Natal in South Africa, died of his wounds in Germany on 11 April 1918. In all about 50 Munsters were killed in action. Among the dead was 2nd Lieutenant Daniel Joseph Mehegan of the 10th Dublins, who was attached to the 2nd Munsters. The Signals Officer, Lieutenant Andrew Strachan, who was reported as missing, was also attached from the Dublins.

The End of the First Day

The elaborate defence strategy had not worked. By 10.30 a.m., most of the Forward Zone had been overrun. The Germans had broken through the Battle Zone in four places, equidistant along the Fifth Army front. There were now gaps at Ronssoy (16th (Irish) and 66th Divisions), Massiemy (24th Division), Essigny (36th (Ulster), 14th and 18th Divisions) and opposite La Fere (58th Division). The Germans had advanced over 6 km into the Fifth Army's southern area.

The soldiers in the forward positions did not have the numbers nor the strong defences to resist the forces sent against them. There were not enough troops positioned in the Battle Zone to repel the enemy who had bypassed the machine gun strong points in the mist. There was little point in using the reserves to regain the Battle Zone now that the size of the German force was known. General Gough ordered a limited withdrawal to the Green Line at 10 p.m. He decided that the most effective tactic was to delay the Germans by rearguard action while maintaining an unbroken line. He ordered that the old French Somme trenches south of the Somme be prepared as a last line of defence [7]. Martin Middlebrook attributes the British failure to four factors: the nature of the defensive system used, the weather conditions on the day, and the morale and the lack of fighting spirit of the British soldiers and the skill of the German infantry [8].

In line with General Gough's new plan, the surviving Dublins would now prepare to resist the enemy in defensive positions north of Tincourt that had not yet been properly prepared.

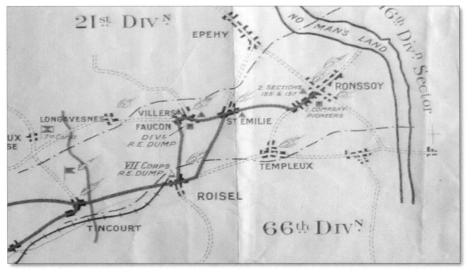

Retreat of 16th (Irish) Division to the Green Line on 21-22 March 1918.
From the War Diary of the Division WO 95/1956

The Commander in Chief sent the following message to the Fifth Army at the end of the first day of the battle:

> *"The C in C sends his congratulations to the troops of your Army on their splendid defence today. He relies on their continued steadfastness and valour to crush this new attack and with it the enemy's last hopes of success."*[9]

The total British losses for the day amounted to about 38,500. Of these, 7,512 had been killed, 10,000 wounded and 21,000 had been taken prisoner. The Germans had 40,000 casualties, of whom 10,851 were killed and 28,778 wounded. [10]. The Germans would find it difficult to replace the experienced soldiers who had been carefully selected and trained to use the new storm-trooper tactics.

A Temporary Victory

The German soldiers who passed through the Irish positions could not have foreseen that the roles would be reversed in the following September when the British recaptured the area as they relentlessly drove the Germans to their final capitulation. On 18 September, the 12th (Eastern) Division attacked the defences around Epehy and retook Malassise Farm after a tough fight. The officer in charge was Major-General Harold Whitla Higginson, a former Royal Dublin Fusilier. He had joined the regiment as a Second Lieutenant in 1894, served during the Boer War and had commanded the 2nd Royal Dublin Fusiliers from June 1915 to May 1916 [11]. The German garrison put up a stubborn defence, inflicting heavy casualties. The Division lost 6,229 officers and men in an advance of 40 km that had begun on 8 August [12]. The Division memorial at the entrance to Malassise Farm, which for many years had been just the base of the original cross, was fully restored in 2007.

The unveiling of the 12th Eastern Division Memorial in front of Malassise Farm, 1921. The Division has a similar memorial at La Chapelle de Feuchy, on the Arras-Cambrai road.

The 2nd Dublins and the 2nd Munsters came back to Epehy and nearby Tetard Wood on 2 October 1918 to prepare to take La Pannerie South, a small village lying about one kilometre north of Le Catelet. The 2nd Munsters were successful after tough street-fighting in Le Catelet on 4 October [13]. This was the third time that the 2nd Dublins had marched through this area.

The only local reminders of the Irish regiments that spent the winter months in the frontline and then fought and died during the March Offensive in the locality are the gravestones in nearby military cemeteries such as Unicorn (Vendhuile), Ste Emilie Valley, Villers Foucon Communal Cemetery Extension, Templeux-Le-Guerard and Epehy Wood Farm Cemetery. St. Patrick's Valley is now just a long forgotten name on an old Trench Map. The Dublin Fusiliers who manned the Forward Zone on the morning of the attack in such a futile role also faded from the collective Irish memory until recent times. The lines from Tennyson's Charge of the Light Brigade make a fitting epitaph for them:

Theirs not to make reply,
Theirs not to reason why,
Theirs but to do and die....

References

(1) Junger, p. 81

(2) Doyle, p.10

(3) War Diary of the 1st Royal Dublin Fusiliers, WO95/1974

(4) War Diary of the 2nd Royal Dublin Fusiliers, W95/1974

(5) War Diary of the 2nd Royal Munster Fusiliers, WO95/1975

(6) Confidential Report by Major M. M. Hartigan, 13 April 1918, WO/1975

(7) Doyle, p.114,

(8) Middlebrook, p.322

(9) Appendix 1/15 Report on the Operations Carried out by the 16th Division, March 21st to March 25th, 1918, W0/1956

(10) Middlebrook, p.328

(11) Simkin, p.18

(12) http://www.1914-1918.net/12div.htm

(13) Jervis, p.52

Chapter 4
The Human Cost

The Human Cost of Delaying the German Attack

The German timetable was disrupted on the first day by stubborn resistance along the front. Despite the intensive shelling, the soldiers manned their posts until they were overwhelmed by the force of numbers. The records show that a total of 162 Dublins were killed on the first day but the true figure may be higher. Accurate record keeping was not a high priority during the fighting retreat. The data held by the Commonwealth War Graves Commission guarantees that the names of those who died will not fade from history but the bare details tell us little about the men involved.

Since its foundation in 1996, the Royal Dublin Fusiliers Association has tried to assemble material to convey something about the people that lie behind the long lists of names on memorials to the missing, such the one for the Fifth Army at Pozieres. The following examples are representative of those who died on the first day of the battle as they tried to do their duty against insuperable odds.

The Pals from Suvla Bay.

Among the Dublin Fusilier casualties on this day were a number of the original members of "D" Company, 7th Battalion, Royal Dublin Fusiliers who were known as "The Pals". When the war broke out, the President of the Irish Rugby Football Union, F H Browning, called for volunteers to form the Irish Rugby Football Union Volunteer Corps. Many joined from other athletic clubs and from business and the professions. Two hundred and eighty six opted for the special company, "D", that was reserved for them in the newly formed 7th (Service) Battalion of the Royal Dublin Fusiliers. After training, they landed at Suvla Bay in Gallipoli on 7 August 1915 where they suffered heavy casualties. When the battalion was withdrawn on 29 September 1915, there were only seventy-nine privates and non-commissioned survivors from the original "D" Company [1]. Many of these, and others who had been withdrawn because of wounds or illness, were subsequently offered commissions and went on to fight on the Western Front. Given their education and background, the volunteers could have applied to become officers at the start but they enlisted as privates so that they could serve together.

Acting Captain David Noel Karney, 2nd Dublins, was one of those killed in action. He was born in Edinburgh but his parents Joseph Braham and Ellen Anne Karney moved to 100 Leinster Road, Rathmines in Dublin. He was educated at the John Ivory School in New Ross and Cork. He was working as a clerk in the Bank of Ireland, College Green Branch in Dublin, when he enlisted. His name is on the bronze memorial in his old workplace. His younger brother, George Wolfe Karney, had also joined "D" Company. Promoted to Lance Corporal, he was killed in action on the Kiretch Tepe Sirt Ridge in Gallipoli on 16 August 1916 when aged 27. He had played international hockey for Ireland in 1914.

Former Members of "D" Company, 7th Dublins

Captain David Karney.

Captain William Kee.

2nd. Lt. Frank Howden.

2nd. Lt. George Clarke.

Another former Pal was Acting Captain William Kee, M.C., 1st Dublins, who was wounded and captured. He was born at Meenagrove, Co Donegal and was educated at Mountjoy School and Trinity College in Dublin. He was a Divinity student when he joined "D" Company. He was immediately elected Sergeant and promoted to Company Sergeant-Major in July 1915, just prior to the landing at Suvla Bay. He was commissioned as a 2nd Lieutenant in charge of "D" Company in September 1915 and wounded in the Macedonian campaign in October 1916. Mentioned in despatches for his "distinguished gallantry in the field at Suvla Bay", he was awarded the Military Cross on 25 November 1916. He died of his wounds in German captivity on 24 March. He was posthumously awarded a Bar to his Military Cross on 16 September 1918 with the following citation:

"For conspicuous gallantry and devotion to duty. This officer displayed the greatest fortitude and much ability in leadership when withstanding, with the company under his command, repeated attacks by the enemy, who were advancing in overwhelming numbers. He continued to fight in the most determined way, refusing to retire until he himself was severely wounded and most of his men had become casualties."

Neither officer has a known grave but they are commemorated on the Pozieres Memorial. William Kee's name is also on the Trinity College Great War Memorial in the 1937 Reading Room on the Front Square.

A third Pal was Second-Lieutenant Frank William Howden, 1st Dublins, aged 26. He was wounded on 21 March and evacuated to the military hospital at Wimereux where he died on 30 March. He is buried in Wimereux Communal Cemetery. The younger son of John and Elizabeth Howden, of Longford, he was educated at Ranelagh School Athlone and was employed as a clerk by the City of Dublin Steam Packet Company. During the Gallipoli campaign, he became ill with typhoid on August 22, 1915 but recovered quickly. He came home at Easter 1917 to receive his Commission and went to France in December. A nurse serving with the Queen Mary Army Auxiliary Corps at Wimereux preserved an album containing a photograph of herself standing beside Frank's gravestone in the cemetery at Wimereux. The old album was found among her possessions after she died but there was no clue as to why she kept it for so long [2].

Another Pal, Second-Lieutenant George Alexander Clarke, 1st Dublins, aged 24, was wounded on this day and died on 24 March. He is buried in Honnechy British Cemetery. He was the second son of Alexander Clarke and Margaret Clarke of 68 Whitworth Road, Drumcondra, Dublin. His elder brother, Thomas, had been killed in action on 13 November 1916, aged 23, at the end of the Battle of the Somme. He was a private in the 10th Dublins and is commemorated on the Thiepval Memorial. A third brother, Newcombe, enlisted in the South Irish Horse in August 1914, when he was 17 and was commissioned into the Royal Irish Fusiliers in June 1917. He was reported as a prisoner of war in June 1918. He survived the war and died in Tavistock, England, in 1977.

As described later, two more Pals were killed later in the retreat on 26 March: Lieutenant William MacHutchison and Sergeant Richard Murphy.

Among those wounded and taken prisoner on this day was Second-Lieutenant James Penrose McCarthy. He was the son of Mr and Mrs R. Hillgrove McCarthy, Woodford House, Listowel, Country Kerry who had three sons and two sons-in-law on active service. Educated at Bishop Foy High School Waterford and Skerries College Dublin, he had worked in the Royal Bank of Ireland before joining "D" Company. He was one of the 79 "Pals" who were still active at the end of the Gallipoli campaign. He survived the battle and the war.

Not Forgotten after Ninety Years

Second Lieutenant Donovan Edward Stanford, 2nd Dublins, was the son of Charles Maurice and Louisa Blanche Stanford, of Braiswick House, Colchester. His younger brother, Alan Kinderly, aged 25, was killed on 19 April 1916 while serving as a private with the 29th Battalion of the Canadian Infantry Division, British Columbia Regiment. Neither has a known grave. Donovan's name is commemorated on the Pozieres Memorial and Alan's name is on the Menin Gate Memorial. Their names are also recorded on the War Memorial in Colchester along with that of a Sybil H Stanford who may have been a sister. According to an article in the Essex County Standard of 13 February 2007, Donovan's and Alan's names were among the four that were being added to the fifty-five already on the local war memorial in Myland. Their names were missed from the original roll of honour.

A Soldier from Carlow

Private Mike Greene

Private Michael (Mike) Greene came from Tullow, County Carlow. Prior to his enlistment in the 8th Dublins in February 1915, he had worked as a housepainter and had married Margaret Neill of Hacketstown around 1903. They had three children; Kathleen, Elizabeth and John (Jack). At 40 years of age, he was one of the older volunteers. He was wounded in the Loos Salient, near Hulluch, where the 16th (Irish) Division suffered 1,980 casualties (570 killed) in the German gas attack 27-29 April 1916. He recovered in time to take part in the fighting at Guillemont in September 1916 and the Battle of Messines in June 1917. Following further action near Langemark and Ypres, Mike was granted home leave in October 1917. A card posted to his wife "Peg" from Southhampton, as he made his way back to Flanders, bore the prophetic phrase "yours till death". In February 1918, Mike was reassigned to the 2nd Dublins during the general reorganisation. He was killed on the first day of the battle and his body was probably not recovered until the area was retaken in September 1918. After the Armistice, the remains were recovered from the surrounding battlefields and Mike was identified and is now buried at Unicorn Cemetery Vendhuille, just east of Ronssoy/Lempire. His wife survived him by 44 years. In 1924, she paid 8 shillings and 2 pence to a have this inscription added to his headstone: *"From his loving wife and children"*.

No. **B 54920**

IMPERIAL WAR GRAVES COMMISSION.

Dear Sir (Madam), Date.....**2 3 JUN 1924**.........192

I am directed by the Imperial War Graves Commission to ask you to be so good as to forward to the **FINANCE DEPARTMENT, Imperial War Graves Commission, 82, Baker Street, London, W. 1**, the sum of...... *8/2d.* ....in payment of the following personal inscription :

....

From his loving wife

and Children

....

consisting of........*28*.............................letters at 3½d. per letter, which will be engraved at your request on the headstone of.*Pte: Michael Greene*...................................

Regiment.*Roy. Dub. Fus.* age.*44?*.in Cemetery '   U N I C O R N   "A"

X   *Cheques, Postal and Money Orders should be crossed and made payable to the Imperial War Graves Commission.*

I am,

You are particularly requested to return this Form with remittance, on receipt of which a formal acknowledgment will be sent to you.   Your obedient Servant,

FABIAN WARE,

Major-General, Vice-Chairman.

mrs Greene, Co. Carlow.

The year of death is incorrectly shown in the Commonwealth War Graves records as 1919. The information and photographs were provided by Michael's grandsons, Frank, Michael and John Greene.

Private Charles Francis McCluskey

Private Charles McCluskey

Private Charles McCluskey was with Captain Karney, "C" Company, 2nd Dublins, in the right front company position. He was 23 years of age and unmarried when he was killed on 21 March. His younger brother, Edward Vincent, served as a 2nd Lieutenant in the Royal Dublin Fusiliers and came through the war safely.

They were the sons of Edward McCluskey, of 74, Hill St., East, Glasgow who was from Dublin. He moved to Glasgow in 1889 before the sons were born. When almost twenty years of age, Edward junior went to the Recruiting Office at 102 Grafton Street in Dublin on 20 June 1916 to join the 10th Royal Dublin Fusiliers. He passed the medical examination and following the instructions of Major Smyth, the recruiting officer, he reported to the Recruiting Office in Glasgow two days later.

2nd Lieutenant Edward McCluskey

He wanted to visit his home before enlisting. Despite his prior arrangement, he was assigned to the 4th Scottish Rifles. He immediately wrote to Major Smyth and his father wrote to John Redmond seeking the transfer. Permission to move to the 11th Dublins at Wellington Barracks in Dublin, was granted by the War Office in London on 17 August 1916. He applied for a temporary commission in December 1916 and was successful. He was wounded during the war and was in hospital in London and Dublin until 1920.

Charles has no known grave and is commemorated on the Pozieres Memorial.

The information was provided by Edward's daughter, Rosemary McLean.

Some Survivors

Sergeant Thomas Cunningham – Taken Prisoner

Sergeant Thomas Cunningham of the 2nd Dublins survived the bombardment and the German assault and was taken prisoner. He was the eldest of nine children and was raised by two grand-aunts. As a painter and decorator, he was a trade union activist during the 1913 General Strike in Dublin. He enlisted in the Royal Dublin Fusiliers at the outbreak of war, promoted to Sergeant within weeks and assigned to administrative duties. His request for active service was granted after the bloodbath of the Somme. He arrived in the 2nd Dublins in time to participate in the 3rd Battle of Ypres, known as Passchendaele.

Tommy Cunningham. seated, first on the right.

Tommy was in the Ridge Reserve trench and saw the Germans bayoneting the prisoners taken in the forward trenches. Rather than retreating, he decided to hold a hand grenade behind his back and prepared to blow up both himself and an attacker. Luckily, a German officer stopped the bayoneting and invited Tommy and his comrades to surrender. He dropped the grenade without being seen and pressed it into the soft mud with his boot. He was transported to a prisoner of war camp in Germany. There, along with thousands of his comrades, he suffered malnutrition on a diet of black bread and imitation coffee, supplemented with nettle and potato skin soup. He was released from the German POW Camp at the end of the war but became a victim of the Spanish Flu epidemic. On 21 August 1920, he was discharged from the army with a note saying he was of *"good character"*.

At the outbreak of In World War Two in 1939, Tommy went to Belfast to re-enlist despite being 54 years old. The recruiting sergeant declined his offer of help and he was sent back to Dublin. In 1964, when Tommy was seventy-nine years of age, he suffered a collapsed lung and was taken to the Adelaide Hospital in Dublin. The night he was admitted, he greeted his fellow patients with 'Hello, I'm Tommy Cunningham and I fought with the Royal Dublin Fusiliers in the First World War.' He died three weeks later.

Tommy's son, Kevin, was proud to relate his father's story.

Mr Kevin Cunningham telling his father's story in front of Malassise Farm during a visit by the Royal Dublin Fusiliers Association in September 2000. Behind him is the plinth of the 12th Eastern Division memorial cross, now restored.

Second Lieutenant William Green, 2nd Battalion

Among those taken prisoner at Enfer Wood at 10 a.m., was Second Lieutenant Greene, 352 North Circular Road, Phibsborough, Dublin. He was marched to Bertry and on the following day to Le Cateau. He was allowed to send official cards to his wife and father before being sent by train to Germany on 24 March. He kept a diary during his imprisonment in the camp at Karlsruhe.

Despite the anguish of the battle and capture, the prisoners adapted quickly to their new circumstances. As early as 6 April, they organised a concert in the camp. On 13 April, Lieutenant Greene took part in a performance of Lady Gregory's *The Rising of the Moon*, the text of which he wrote down from memory. One of the actors was Lieutenant John Martin, a Royal Dublin Fusilier Officer who was attached to the Royal Inniskillings when he was captured. He had been a successful actor with the Abbey Theatre under the stage name Philip Guiry before the war broke out. There were many further concerts in the camp. The prisoners had a piano and gramophone. One month after his capture, William noted in his diary that the time had passed quickly. After the armistice, he returned to his regiment and was notified of his demobilisation on 9 November 1921.

The Information was provided by Mr Pat Power, Arklow.

Sergeant Ned Brierley, Serial Number 20041, Military Medal

Private Edward Brierley was engaged in building the defences behind the lines when the attack began. Born in Ballsbridge, Dublin in 1896, he left his employment with Pembroke District Council to enlist in the 8th Dublins when the war broke out.

He was awarded the Military Medal on 19 November 1917. He received three citations, known as "Hickie Parchments", while serving with the 16th (Irish) Division. The first was for his bravery at Guillemont in September 1916. He was awarded the second for Wijtschaete/Messines and the Frezenberg Ridge in 1917.

He kept a small pocket diary during his period of service. The entry for Thursday, March 21st, states: *"Offensive started, held Brown Line until 11:00 pm from 5:30am."*

He survived the retreat and took part in the final advance against the Germans during which he won his third parchment, illustrated on the opposite page. He was transferred to the Royal Engineers near the end of 1918 and became "Sapper". After demobilisation, he returned to Dublin and to his old job. He married Mary Hayden at St. Joseph's, Glasthule, Co. Dublin, on September 17th, 1924.They had seven children, one of whom, Noel, said, "My father was a very quiet, hard working man who never spoke about his experiences in the war."

He played football with Shelbourne A.F.C. during 1925/26 and with St. Mary's United A.F.C. in the Leinster Football League. He won a runners-up medal playing for St. Mary's in the Edmund Johnson Cup and the following season, a runners-up medal in the Metropolitan Cup.

Edward died from a heart attack while working, on November the 23rd 1955.

The information about this veteran Royal Dublin Fusilier was provided to Tom Burke by his sons, Noel and the late Edward who died in May 2005.

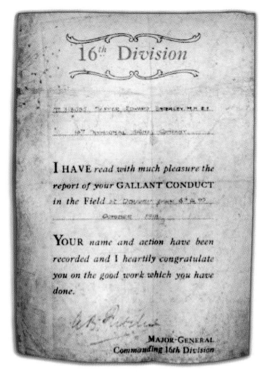

The Grim Total

The records show that two Captains, nine Second Lieutenants and 162 NCOs and men from the 1st and 2nd Dublins were killed on 21 March. The 2nd Dublins lost 117 soldiers, more than double the losses from the first battlalion. Eighty per cent of those who died have no known grave and are commemorated on the Pozieres Memorial. The Germans made three large mass graves in what is now Ste. Emilie Valley Cemetery, Villers-Faucon. This cemetery also has 222 unidentified graves.

It is probable that some of those who are recorded as having died later in the retreat were also killed on the first day of the battle. The bodies of some who were killed on 29 March are buried in cemeteries close to the positions on 21 March.

Three other officers who were wounded on this day, died later. Second Lieutenant Reuben H. Howell, 2nd Dublins, died on 29 March and is buried in St Sever Cemetery, Rouen. This city was a major hospital centre for the duration of the war. Second Lieutenant Robert Percy Ellis, of the same battalion, was wounded, captured and died on 6 April. He is buried in Hautmont Communal Cemetery. This town was captured by the Germans at the start of the war and it remained in their hands until it was retaken on 8 November 1918. He was the eldest son of William H Ellis, King Edward Terrace, Drumcondra. He enlisted in March 1915 and served in France and Salonika before receiving his commission in the Royal Dublin Fusiliers in November 1917.

Second Lieutenant Ronald Gordon Hunter, 19, 1st Dublins, was captured and died of his wounds on 25 April. He was the second son of William and Helen Hunter of Baymount, Sutton, Co. Dublin. A newspaper report on 4 May stated that he was a wounded prisoner in Germany [5]. In 1922, it was decided that the graves of Commonwealth servicemen who had died as prisoners in Germany should be brought together into four permanent cemeteries. Berlin South-Western was one of those chosen and, in 1924-25, remains were brought from more than 140 burial grounds in eastern Germany. Ronald now lies in this cemetery. He is named on the memorial in Clontarf Presbyterian Church, Howth Road.

The two Company Sergeant Majors from the 2nd Dublins, Walter John Morley and William Bethel Fox who were killed, have no known grave and are commemorated on the Pozieres Memorial.

Two of the remaining officers from the 1st Dublins listed in the War Diary as missing on 21 March were Acting-Captain G. H. Chandler, MC, (wounded) and Acting-Captain H. M. Letchworth [6]. Their names do not appear on the Commonwealth War Graves Commission website nor on the Roll of Honour in Neill's "Blue Caps" which suggests that they survived the war. Despite Captain Letchworth's final defiant message as recorded in the War Diary and referred to earlier, it is probable that he was forced to surrender.

Second-Lieutenant James Nolan, MC, DCM, was wounded but managed to avoid capture. He recovered and returned to active service with the 1st Dublins. Later that year, on 29 September, he was killed in a major attack on the German positions near Poperinghe in Belgium and is buried in Birr Cross Roads Cemetery.

Corporal Henry White of the 2nd Dublins was awarded the Military Medal on 13 March, "for bravery in the Field" just eight days before he was killed [7]. He was from Newcastle, Kilcoole, Co Wicklow.

Corporal Michael Mahon, 11714, aged 22, from Ballymore Eustace, Co Kildare was among those reported missing. He was taken prisoner and was shot and killed on 31 August while trying to escape. He has no known grave and is commemorated on the Pozieres Memorial.

Twenty-two year-old Sergeant George Frederick Batwell, 2nd Dublins, appears to have been an only brother to six sisters. The one Batwell family living in Dublin when the 1911 Census was taken resided at 95 Circular Road, Portobello. The parents were James and Mary and their youngest child was named George, then aged 14. James was an army pensioner. His children had been born in England, Galway, the West Indies, Canada as well as in Dublin.

The Dublins who managed to survive the first day of the battle still had many tough days ahead before they would reach safety.

References

(1) Henry Hanna, The Pals at Suvla Bay, E. Ponsonby Ltd, Dublin, 1917.
(2) Correspondence with a relative of the nurse. The picture was spotted in the album after her death. The headstones were not erected until after the war.
(3) The Roll of Honour is now in St. Thomas's Church, Cathal Brugha Street, Dublin 1.
(4) Correspondence with nephew
(5) Irish Times, 4 May 1918
(6) War Diary 1st Battalion, The Royal Dublin Fusiliers, WO95/1974
(7) London Gazette, issue 30573, 13 March.1918.

Chapter 5
The Retreat

The Retreat

The German successes on the opening day of the offensive sent shockwaves as far as the Cabinet Office in Downing Street. The previous costly Allied failures at the Somme in 1916 and at Passchendaele in 1917 had made it seem unlikely that either side could succeed in a breakthrough. But now the elaborate defensive strategy had failed to halt the enemy soldiers who could recover the territory so dearly won in the previous two years. The apportionment of blame became an issue but that was secondary to the need for emergency action. Over the next few days, major changes were made, the most important of which was the appointment of a supreme Allied Commander, Marshal Foch. The reserves which Lloyd George had withheld were now released.

The individual soldiers who survived the opening day of the attack knew that there was no real prospect of stopping the German advance with the resources then available. Safety lay somewhere in the west and the remaining Dublins became part of the columns trying to find a safe route through the familiar, though ravaged, landscape. Over the next eight days and nights they took up a number of defensive positions and then quickly moved on. They eventually reached the village of le Hamel where they were relieved.

Some of the veteran 2nd Dublins may have recalled a similar experience during the German initial advance in August 1914 when they marched through Le Catelet down the road to Roisel.

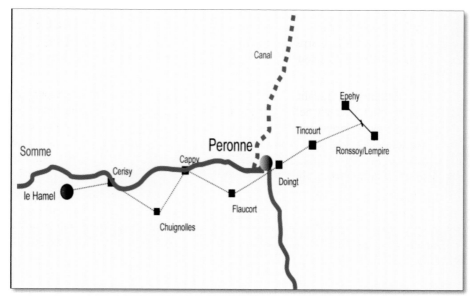

Route taken by the 1st and 2nd Dublins 21 March to 29 March 1918

The following chronology of the retreat is based on the details in the relevant War Diaries, Neill's "Blue Caps", Crown and Company, individual case histories and other published material included in the bibliography. There are some understandable discrepancies in dates and places, given the confused circumstances and the numbers of casualties and prisoners taken.

The Second Day of the Retreat: 22 March

As dawn broke, the 2nd Dublins were ordered to fall back to the old Divisional Headquarters at **Villers Foucon.** When this was reached, they were ordered to continue on to **Tincourt** which the 1st Dublins had reached at 4 a.m. The soldiers now had their first proper meal since the 20th. Only five officers and ninety other ranks had made it this far. Along with the Royal Munster Fusiliers, they took up position for the night along the road running north-west from Tincourt. They were now in support of the Green Line and made all the necessary arrangements to engage the advancing Germans there.

The Germans renewed their attack at 10.30 am. The 1st Dublins, about 140 strong, were ordered to occupy the Green Line with its right flank at **Hamel.** This is about 1km to the east of **Tincourt** and is not the same town as le Hamel where the retreat ended. The Germans pressed their attack to the right of the battalion. At 3 p.m., the 50th Division made a counter attack on the battalion's right in the vicinity of **Roisel.** There was no action on the battalion's front during the day. The line was held until the following morning.

Orders were issued and countermanded during the day. At 4.15 p.m., an order was issued for VII Corps to withdraw to the Green line at 8 p.m. This was cancelled at 6.15 p.m. At 9.25 p.m., VII Corps was ordered to withdraw to the Doingt/Bois Des Flaques/East of Bussu Aizecourt/Nurlu/Equancourt Line. This order was cancelled at 10.10 p.m.

The 19th Entrenching Battalion moved on from **Vraignes-en-Vermandois** eastwards to **Vermand** which was reached at 1 a.m. They took up a defensive line in front of the village. In the early forenoon, the Germans were seen advancing in large numbers. The defenders inflicted heavy losses with rifle fire but the Germans began to bypass the resistance. Seeing this, half of the battalion was withdrawn. The other half was assigned to the command of the 24th Division.

There is a list of those killed in Appendix A. Of the six killed in action on 22 March, two were from the 2nd Dublins, one from the 1st and three from the 10th. The latter were probably serving with the 19th Entrenching Battalion. Private Patrick Finegan is buried in Ennemain Communal Cemetery which is situated 10 km south-south-east of Peronne. The other two have no known graves.

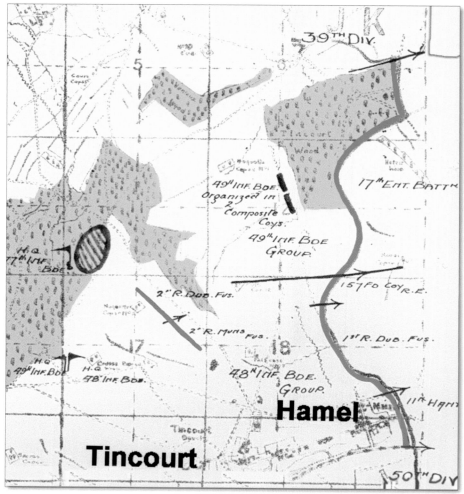

Green Line position on 22 March. Adapted from WO 95/1956

The Third Day: 23 March

The day began with another very heavy mist that restricted visibility to about 50 metres. To take advantage of the fog, the 2nd Dublins were ordered to support a general retreat through **Courcelles** to a position at the Bois des Flaques covering **Bussu** and **Peronne**. They began to fall back at 7am using a compass to guide direction and supported by tanks. The new position was a line from **Doingt to Bussu** which was reached without incident.

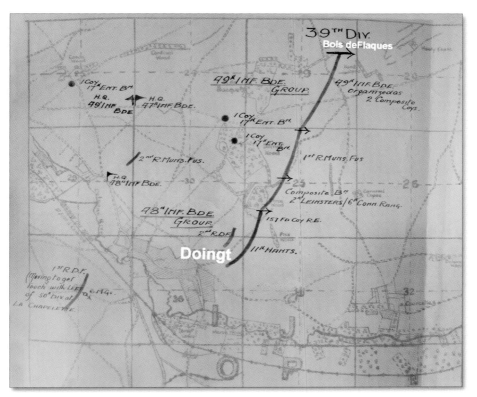

Disposition on the Doingt-Bois de Flaque Line at 10.30 am on 23 March.
Adapted from WO 95/1956.

The 1st Dublins arrived at 11 a.m. and became the Brigade Reserve. At about 1 p.m., they moved south of **Doingt** and took up a position about 1.5 km south east of **Peronne** to cover the withdrawal of the Brigade across the Somme if that became necessary. At about 2 p.m., the Battalion was ordered to cross the river to take up a position at **la Maisonnette** which was on a height overlooking **Peronne** and **Biaches**, the next town to the west. Some soldiers were sent further west to a position 3 km east of **Flaucourt.**

The town of Biaches as destroyed by the Germans during the 1917 fallback.

The Germans attacked the 2nd Battalion's position but were repulsed. The battalion then moved to a location west of **Peronne**. When it arrived there at about 3 p.m., it was ordered to hold the bridgehead as long as possible. The brigades to their left and right had been driven over the Somme.

At 10.30 p.m., the remains of the 16th (Irish) Division were instructed to march 11km from **Biaches** to **Cappy** to form a reserve. The retreat was without panic. Hot tea was provided for the men on the route and when they arrived at **Cappy** at 4 a.m., there was a hot meal. There was no trace of the platoon from the 2nd Dublins that had courageously remained on the other side of the river to cover the crossing of the bridge at Peronne.

The loss of Peronne was a serious blow. The failure to stop the Germans at the River Somme gave the advancing troops access to an area containing hospitals and large quantities of abandoned stores. The sick and wounded were evacuated in very difficult conditions.

The 19th Entrenching Battalion moved to **Devise** where a line was dug. At about 10 a.m., retreating British troops passed through the line. The Germans advanced over open country preceded by small detachments of machine gunners. When they were held up, they found a gap on the right where the British had retired. As there was a risk of being surrounded, the 19th withdrew to **St Christ.** They were assigned to the 24th Division and moved to **Pressoire.** Three soldiers of the 10th Battalion were killed in action. The casualties recorded for this day were again light. Seven have no known grave and are commemorated on the Pozieres Memorial. Company Sergeant Major William Henry Davies, 28238, formerly of the 8/9th Battalion and the 11th (Prince Albert's Own) Hussars, was killed in action. He came from Edgbaston in Warwickshire.

Private J McCaffrey, 1ˢᵗ Battalion, was also killed in action, but his remains were found and he is buried in Brie British Cemetery. He is the only soldier of the 16th (Irish) Division buried in this Cemetery. Brie is a village on the main Amiens to St. Quentin road (N29), south of Peronne. The area and its bridge were captured by the Germans on 23 March. The 19ᵗʰ Entrenching Battalion had come under fire along the Vermand–Brie Road on the previous day. It is possible that Private McCaffrey was with this battalion, along with others from the 10ᵗʰ Dublins.

The casualties for the 16ᵗʰ (Irish) Division since the start of the battle amounted to 203 Officers and 5,340 Other Ranks.

The Fourth Day: 24 March

The 1ˢᵗ and 2ⁿᵈ Dublins were allowed to rest in **Cappy**, until about 4.30 p.m. when the 1ˢᵗ marched on to **Froissy.** The 2ⁿᵈ followed, having gathered a few reinforcements and those available from the Transport unit to form four "very weak" companies with 7 officers and 120 NCOs and men. They marched to **Froissy** on the canal, south of Bray, where they took up positions on the southern bank to guard the bridge against an attack from the south. The 2ⁿᵈ Munsters were on the right and the 1ˢᵗ Dublins were in support. The night passed without incident. The 20ᵗʰ Entrenching Battalion left their camps and kit behind when they moved off for **Harbonnieres.**

The five Dublins who died on this day, did so from wounds. Captain Kee and Lt. Clarke, were wounded on 21 March, as described in Chapter 4. Corporal Rafferty is buried in Ribemont Cemetery which is 8 km south west of Albert, a good distance from the position on 24 March. He is the only Dublin among the 462 buried there. The officers do not appear to have had any information on the progress being made by the Germans to the north or south. The various defensive lines envisaged by the strategists before the Offensive do not appear to have played an important role during the retreat.

The Fifth Day: 25 March

As a consequence of a reorganisation intended to allow General Gough to concentrate on the area south of the Somme, the 16ᵗʰ Division was ordered to retrace its steps to a position east of **Cappy** to cover the Somme bridgehead. At about 3 pm, the two battalions marched east to **Eclusier** to guard the bridge against an attack from the north. The Royal Engineers blew it up at 1 am. That was the only thing to disturb the sleep that night. The 20ᵗʰ Entrenching Battalion had a fight with the Germans on the way to **Harbonnieres** in which four privates from the 8/9ᵗʰ Dublins were killed. They have no known grave.

Captain Cyril Bernard Donovan, MC, is recorded as having been killed in action on this day while serving with the 2ⁿᵈ Dublins. He had received his Military Cross on 1 January 1918. His name is on the war memorial in Hertford. It is possible that he was with the 20ᵗʰ Entrenching Battalion at the time of his death.

Private Patrick Savage from Blackburn died in Amiens on this day. He was serving with the 10th Dublins. His brother Peter had been killed in action on 13 November 1916 at Beaumont Hamel while serving in the same battalion.

The Sixth Day: 26 March

As the day dawned, the troops in the front positions began to retire in the face of what appeared to be a strong attack by the Germans. There was a general withdrawal towards **Chuignolles** to form part of the **Bray-Proyart** Line. By 9 am, the 1st Battalion was in the Brigade Reserve at the crossroads 3 km east of **Mericourt** and about 1.5 kms to the rear of the line. When the 2nd Battalion arrived, they began to dig positions between the cemetery south of **Chuignolles** and **Proyart**. It had a battalion of Munster Fusiliers on either side.

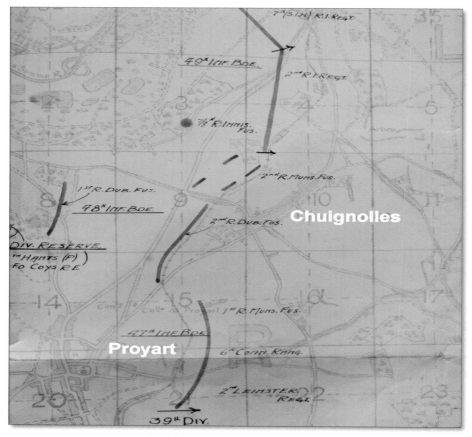

Position at 2.30 p.m. on 26 March.
Adapted from WO 95/ 1956

They were barely in position when, at about 2.30 pm, a strong German attack was launched, supported by heavy artillery. **Chuignolles** was captured. There was severe fighting until the left flank was turned, and at about 5pm, the 2nd Dublins were forced to withdraw and take up a position in an old French trench system between **Mericourt** and **Chuignolles**. They were on the forward slope of the hill facing east with a thick copse on the right. The 47th Brigade was to the right but contact could not be made. The 1st Dublins allowed the 2nd Royal Irish Regiment to withdraw through their position and held on until dark. It then withdrew to the Brigade Reserve position on the heights south east of **Mericourt**.

A Change in Command

The German offensive had now driven the Allies behind the line from which they had launched the Battle of the Somme on July 1, 1916. There was a real risk that the attack would succeed in reaching the coast and dividing the French and British Armies, each of which could be dealt with in turn. A top level meeting was held in the town hall at Doullens which was General Byng's HQ. The French participants included President Poincaré, Prime Minister Clemenceau and Marshal Foch, Chief of the French General Staff. The British side had Lord Milner from the War Cabinet, General Sir Henry Wilson and Douglas Haig. Marshal Foch was given overall command of the Allied armies on the Western Front. The Commanders-in-Chief of the British, French and US armies retained the right to appeal to his government in the event of a disagreement.

Foch decided that the Germans had to be stopped in front of Amiens. He agreed to make French reserves available. The retreat must stop. He went to General Gough's HQ to express his dissatisfaction with the performance of the Fifth Army. The line was to be held at all costs.

The Entrenching Battalions

The 20th Entrenching Battalion was ordered to join the 16th (Irish) Division and it moved towards **Bray sur Somme** before arriving at **Etineham.**

Royal Dublin Fusilier Captain Robert Boyd, aged 28, was in charge of "C" Company of the 19th Entrenching Battalion at **Hattencourt**, a small town just north of **Roye**. As the only Captain in the line, he was put in charge of the four companies that had been ordered to dig a trench about 50 metres east of the town about 2 a.m. The work had been completed when the Germans attacked at 6.30 a.m. Captain Boyd was ordered to hold the line at all costs. At 7.15 a.m., he received a written instruction to withdraw and join the 16th (Irish) Division. Two of the four companies had got away under covering fire when he was hit on the side of the head by a piece of mortar shrapnel that pierced his helmet. When he recovered consciousness, a German was applying a field dressing. The "Good Samaritan" had already taken his revolver, field glasses and wristwatch. He survived and was repatriated in December 1918 [1].

He was the son of Rev. Robert Boyd of Gujerat in India and had been the President of the Philosophical Society in Trinity College, Dublin before joining the Malay Branch of the Indian Civil Service. On the outbreak of the war, he returned to take a Commission in the Royal Dublin Fusiliers. After the war he resumed his career, becoming the Director of Co-Operation, Federated Malay States and Straits Settlements in 1933. He was a civilian prisoner of war during the Second World War. Awarded the CMG in 1946, he died in Belfast on 2 March1976 [2]. The confusion of the retreat led to a report in the Irish Times of 27 April 1918 that Captain Boyd had been killed in action. The same paper published the notice of his actual death almost 58 years later.

Two More "Pals"

The records show that two former Pals were killed on this day. Sergeant Richard Victor Murphy was the second son of Mr and Mrs W A Murphy, Borris, County Carlow. He was educated at Kilkenny, Portarlington and Mountjoy School, Dublin and became a Civil Servant in the Land Registry in Dublin. He joined the Pals battalion in September 1914 and served with them in Gallipoli and Serbia before being invalided home in July 1916. He recovered and went to France in July 1917. He was invalided home again with pneumonia. He returned to the front in January 1918. He had been a member of Wanderers Rugby Football Club. His name is on the brass memorial in the Land Registry along with that of Francis H. Browning, the President of the Irish Rugby Football Union who was killed in Dublin in 1916 on the first day of the Easter Rising.

Sergt. Richard V. Murphy

Lieut. William F. MacHutchison

Lieutenant William F. MacHutchison was the son of John MacHutchison of 5 Orwell Park , Dublin. He attended St Andrews School before entering the Hong Kong and Shanghai Banking Corporation. He joined the Pals and served in Gallipoli before being sent to hospital in Giza, Egypt, in August 1915.

He resumed active service in October 1915 and became the Quartermaster-Sergeant of the 30th Infantry Brigade before accepting his Commission in May 1916. The following October, he was almost killed in an action in the Struma Valley when a rifle bullet went through his chest just above his heart. Though seriously wounded, he recovered and was sent home to Dublin to recuperate in December. He was declared fit for service abroad in May 1917.

His parents, who were living at 6 Mount Temple Terrace, Dartry Road, Dublin, were notified of his death in April 1918. The recorded date is 26 March but this may be incorrect. (Captain Leonard Sheridan's date may also be wrongly recorded as discussed below). A fellow officer wrote that William was wounded in the head by a machine gun bullet on the afternoon of 27 March. Two soldiers were directed to take him to the nearest Field Ambulance which was in the village of Lamotte. At the time it was not known that the village had been captured by the Germans and wounded men were sent there all that evening and night. The German Medical Officer, who had taken over the station, sent a report that William had died there after two days, but apparently that report and all the other papers were captured by the Germans and were lost [3].

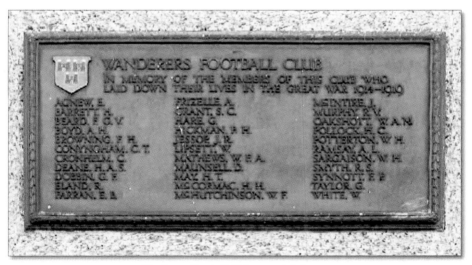

Wanderers Football Club memorial plaque.
From www.irishwarmemorials.ie

The names of Lieutenant MacHutchison and Sergeant Murphy are on the memorial plaque at Lansdowne Road. It also includes the name of Lieutenant Hebron Barrett who was to die on the following day while serving with the 19th Entranching Battalion. The eager recruits who assembled on the pitch at Lansdowne Road in 1914 had no inkling of the ordeals that they would have to face before making the ultimate sacrifice.

2nd. Lieut. Joseph Lowe.

Second-Lieutenant Joseph Lowe, MM, was the son of Mr and Mrs F. J. Lowe, 3 Hollybank Road, Drumcondra and the husband of Mrs S. J. Lowe, 19 Claude Road, Drumcondra, Dublin. He was a Law Clerk in 1911 with a daughter and two sons. He served with the 8th Dublins before his transfer to the 1st. He is commemorated on the Pozieres Memorial.

Second-Lieutenant Thomas Laurence Cahill, MM. was the son of John and Catherine Cahill, Poplar Square, Naas, Co. Kildare. He had enlisted in the 2nd Irish Guards in January 1915 and was wounded in January 1916. He was commissioned into the 8th Dublins in 1917. His name is also on the Pozieres Memorial.

Company Sergeant Major Leo Whittaker, MM, 9709, former 8/9th Battalion, age 36, was one of the eight children of James and Theresa Whitaker, 4 Tramway Terrace Golden Bridge, Inchicore. He is commemorated on the Pozieres Memorial.

None of those killed in action on this day has a known grave.

The German Cemetery at Proyart.

The Seventh Day: 27 March

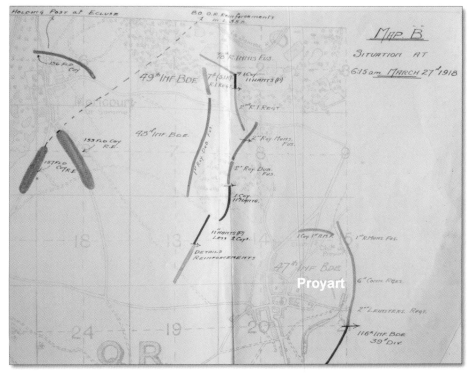

Situation at 6.15 am on 27 March. WO 95/ 1956

The Germans began to shell the positions at daybreak. Large enemy reinforcements were seen but the attacks from the directions of **Chuignolles** and **Proyart** were held back by rifle, artillery and machine-gun fire. The Royal Flying Corps gave valuable assistance. Three German pieces of artillery were put out of action. Despite this, the enemy began to drive back the troops on the right flank. Major Wheeler ordered the 2nd Dublins to "hold on and fight to the last". By the afternoon, it became evident that they and the 2nd Munsters were in danger of being surrounded. Majors Wheeler and Rye (Munsters) decided to withdraw, as remaining in position would serve no useful purpose. As darkness fell, the men left their trenches and passed through **Morcourt,** to reach the bridge at **Ecluse** at 8pm. They found the north side of the bridge occupied by the enemy. They retraced their steps in the dark through **Morcourt** which was in flames, and went along the south bank of the canal to the bridge at **Cérisy**. The troops moving about here were identified as Germans. It was decided to rush the bridge. Major Wheeler's batman was a heavyweight boxer who had recently won a divisional contest. He was placed at the head of the column without his rifle.

The Germans did not challenge them until they had come within 15 metres. Byrne knocked a German out with each fist and revolvers were used to kill two more sentries. The remaining Germans vanished and the column moved towards the location of a British heavy gun that was shelling **Cerisy**. They surprised and killed the German sentries at the next village, **Sailly-Laurette**. They skirted the village fearing that it was full of Germans and went south to the village of l**e Hamel** where they arrived at about 2 a.m. on 28 March. They had marched for some 20 km through the German lines.

The survivors from the 2nd Dublins were Major Wheeler, Captain Stitt, Lieutenant Beaumont and 44 NCOs and men. They had brought about 250 officers and men with them, the remnants of other units.

Once again, the 1st Dublins remained in position to cover the withdrawal. It then moved back to take up a position in the sunken road from **Morcourt** to **Cerisy** at about 5 p.m. About 15 minutes later, the Germans crossed the bridge at **Cerisy** and attacked from the rear. The battalion had to withdraw south to the main road from Peronne to Amiens, east of Lamotte. Stragglers from the 16th, 39th and 66th Divisions were organised to make a counter attack. They went forward for about 1.5km but had to withdraw at about 7pm as there was no support on either side and they were enfiladed by machine-gun fire. They were unable to contact the rest of the brigade and withdrew across country to **Villers Bretonneux,** between **Lamotte** and **Bayonvillers**. They arrived at 11.30 p.m.

At about 9 a.m., the 19th Entrenching Battalion counter attacked and recaptured the village of **Rouvroy-en-Santerre** The Germans attacked again in the afternoon and the battalion had many casualties. It was forced back to a line immediately behind the village where there were some old trenches. During the night there were many enemy patrols, some of whom were captured. The line was accidentally shelled by British heavy artillery when it got dark.

Lieutenant Samuel William Palmer, formerly of the 10th Dublins was serving with the 19th Entrenching Battalion when he was killed in action. He was twenty-two years old. His older brother, Captain David Adams Palmer, MC, formerly of the 3rd Dublins, had died from wounds just two days earlier. Aged twenty-five, he was serving with the Tank Corps. They were the sons of Mr and Mrs David Palmer, Tandragee, Co. Armagh. Their mother died in the following July aged 50. A sad example of the long shadow cast by the Great War. Lieutenant Hebron Barrett died of his wounds and is buried in Namps-au-Val British Cemetery where the 41st, 50th and 55th Casualty Clearing Stations were located during the March Offensive. Both had previously served in the 10th Dublins. In all, eight former members of the 10th Dublins were killed in the fighting. Only Lieutenant Barrett has a known grave.

> **Erected in Loving Memory**
> **of**
> **Capt. David Adams Palmer MC**
> **who died of wounds**
> **received in action in France**
> **on March 25th 1918 in his 25th year**
> **also his brother**
> **Lieut. Samuel William Palmer**
> **who died in France**
> **on March 27th 1918 in his 22nd year**
> **and their mother**
> **Mary Palmer**
> **who peacefully passed away**
> **on July 7th 1918 in her 50th year**
> **also their father**
> **David Palmer**
> **who passed away**
> **on the 13th October 1948**

Headstone inscription at the Presbyterian Church, Tandragee,
Co. Armagh, Northern Ireland. From the Sinton Family Tree website.

Lieutenant Frank Laird's Experience

Lieutenant Frank Laird

In his memoirs, Lieutenant Frank Laird describes how he had been temporarily attached to the 20th Entrenching Battalion near **Peronne**, installing light railways, when the battle had begun [4]. He managed to trek across country and got to the village of **Harbonniéres** which was south of the Peronne-Amiens road before he was ordered to join the remnants of the 16th (Irish) Division. His group spent 36 hours searching for the 1st and 2nd Dublins which were reported to be at **Cappy**. They marched to **Lamotte** on the first day and towards **Bray-Sur-Somme** on the next.

They found the village of **Etinehem** abandoned and were ordered by a General go back across the Somme. On the 27th, near the village of **Morcourt**, a major of the 16th (Irish) Division assigned the group to positions on a bluff commanding the crossroads with orders to remain until the last of the troops had passed through. Lieutenant Laird and another 2nd Lieutenant had about 20 men. He describes the German method of advance as shelling each ridge in succession and pushing their soldiers forward in small parties covered by machine-gun fire. German planes flew very low, peppering the British soldiers and spotting for the artillery. A shell knocked out three soldiers, one of whom died. The group began to retreat when they met a major of the Hampshire Regiment and a captain from the Dublin Fusiliers who were organising a counter attack. [This appears to be the attack by the 1st Dublins already mentioned above.] About 150 advanced in a line across open ground, led by the two officers. They came under artillery and machine-gun fire and Lieutenant Laird was hit. The whistle in his breast pocket deflected the bullet. He was taken prisoner as was another Dublin Fusilier officer named Briscoe. [Second Lieutenant W.R. Briscoe is shown as missing on the 27th in the 1st Dublins' War Diary]. As he passed along the road to **Bray-Sur-Somme**, Frank saw the British dead "lying here and there still unburied".

A graduate of Trinity College, Lieutenant Laird was 35 when he left his Civil Service post to join D Company of the 7th Dublins. One of his instructors was William Kee. They both had survived the Gallipoli campaign. As mentioned earlier, Captain Kee died from the wounds received on 21 March. Frank Laird survived his period as a prisoner in Germany but died as a result of his wounds in 1925.

Captain George Evelyn Cowley was wounded and taken prisoner in the above attack. He subsequently died from his wounds on 18 June 1918 and is buried in Le Cateau Military Cemetery. In a response to a request for information, Lieutenant Laird wrote on 3 March 1919 that he had taken part in a counter attack with Captain Cowley at Morcourt on 27 March 1918 that was halted by machine gun fire. Virtually everyone was hit. He did not see Captain Cowley again, being hit himself [5]. Private. T. Walsh, No. 25666, saw Captain Cowley wounded and left behind on the 26 March 1918 [6].

Captain Cowley had a distinguished military career, being twice mentioned in despatches. He had served in Gallipoli. Before the war he wrote several short stories, occasionally under the pseudonym' Duxmia', which were published in various periodicals, and worked as a cinematographer during the Balkan war of 1912. He married Ida Lencione shortly before his death in 1918. She was living in Ramleh, Alexandria, when he was killed. His papers are held in Nottingham University Library, Department of Manuscripts and Special Collections.

2nd Lieutenant George Perry Crawford, 5 Cambridge Villas, Rathmines, Dublin was also wounded and taken prisoner. His father was officially notified that this occurred while he was engaged in a counter attack on the 27th March. [7]

Major Squire Duff-Taylor, the acting Brigade Major of the 48th Brigade was taken prisoner. He had been commissioned into the 4th Dublins in 1914, transferred to the 2nd Dublins as adjutant in 1916. He was repatriated in December 1918.

Captain Leonard Sheridan

Captain Leonard Sheridan.

Captain Leonard Sheridan, formerly of the East Lancs, had joined the 2nd Dublins on 10 February when the 8/9th was disbanded. He date of death is officially recorded as 26 March but Captain Darling, of the 1st Dublins, wrote a letter on 5 August 1919 to the husband of Leonard's sister Hope, giving details of the death:

"We did not meet again until the 27th, if I remember correctly, on this occasion it was in the vicinity of Morcourt. During the day we had been driven back to the Amiens-Peronne road , near La Motte. It was while we were again retreating that I again met Sherry (Captain Sheridan). We were holding the high ground east of Morcourt Wood under a regular hail of machine gun and rifle bullets, when an officer in a British warm unconcernedly approached me. It was Sherry, he was cheerful as usual, but at the same time one could see that the strain of it all was beginning to tell. He looked very tired and seemed to ignore the deadly fire we were subjected to. We talked together for a time and I remember our parting well. He just said "Cheerio, old bean, I'll see you later" and sauntered down the hill with his hands in the pockets of his British warm. That was the last time I saw poor Sherry alive".[8]

Later that night he heard that Leonard had been killed. Somebody saw him lying with a bullet through his head.

He was the son of John and Ellen Sheridan, proprietors of the Slievmore Hotel, Dugort, Achill. His older brother, Richard, aged 26, was accidentally killed on 7 March 1916 during a grenade training exercise in the Loos sector. Richard is buried in Lillers Communal Cemetery but Leonard has no known grave and is commemorated on the Pozieres Memorial. They had four sisters.

2nd Lt. James Rogers

2nd. Lieutenant James Rogers.

Among those killed in action on 27 March was the twenty seven year old 2nd Lieutenant James Joseph Rogers, 2nd Dublins, who came from Fallagher, Sixmilecross, County Tyrone. In 1910, he passed the entrance examination for Teacher Training and then joined the Royal Irish Constabulary. He was based in Greystones when he enlisted in the 2rd Irish Guards in February 1915. He was quickly promoted to Corporal on December 1915. He was a Lance Sergeant when he received a commission as a 2nd Lieutenant in the 11th Dublins in January 1917. While recovering from a bullet wound in the arm in England, he met a local girl, Fanny Rebecca, whom he married in June 1917. They lived at 74 Crescent Road, Brentwood, Essex.

During the retreat, he was buried in an isolated grave 1 km south of **Sailly Laurette**. When the war was over, his body was recovered, identified and reburied in Heath Cemetery, Harbonnieres in November 1919. This was a concentration cemetery that was used for the identified and unidentified bodies recovered in the surrounding area. (An unknown soldier of the Leicester Regiment was found at the same location.) It contains the grave of an "Unknown Sergeant Major of the Royal Dublin Fusiliers". It is possible that he was Company Sergeant Major James Farrell, 8694, formerly of the 10th Battalion, aged 33, who was also killed on the 27th in this area. He was the son of Charles and Margaret Farrell, Kilbeggan, Co. Westmeath. His name is on the Pozieres Memorial along with five other Sergeant Majors who have no known grave.

They are:

William Bethel Fox	2nd Bn	Killed in action on 21 March.
Walter John Morley	2nd Bn	Killed in action on 21 March.
William Henry Davies	8/9th Bn	Killed in action on 23 March.
Leo Whittaker	8/9th Bn	Killed in action on 26 March.
Joseph Hughes	1st Bn	Killed in action on 29 March.

Links with Darwen, Lancashire

Another who was killed in action on this day was Richard Thomas Eccles, 1st Dublins, who was born in Darwen, Lancashire. He enlisted in Barrow. He may have known the three other 2nd Dublins from the same town who were killed on 21 March. Richard was the son of Christopher and Jane Ann Eccles of 13 Nicholas St., Darwen.

Other Darwen men who were killed while serving with the Dublins are;

> Owen Bolan, 6th Bn, died of wounds on 18 August 1915.
> Herbert Ainsworth, 2nd Bn, killed in action on 21 March 1918.
> Richard Herbert Eccles, 2nd Bn, killed in action on 21 March 1918.
> Walter Taylor, 2nd Bn, killed in action on 21 March1918.
> William Leach Fielden, 10th Bn, died of wounds on 10 April 1918.

A list of Darwen prisoners of war which was published a local paper in August 1920, listed seven who were in the Royal Dublin Fusiliers .[9] *Ireland's Memorial Records* (1923) lists thirty-one Darwen men who were killed while serving in the Irish Regiments. Not all are included on the Darwen Roll of Honour which appears to have been published in 1929 when the Roll of Honour Memorial in nearby Blackburn was unveiled.

Preparing to make a stand

On 23 March, General Gough had begun to assemble a force of some 3,000 soldiers on the Amiens Defence Line located east of **Villers-Bretonneux**. Under the Command of Major General George Carey, they were mainly from engineering, tunnelling and signal companies and included 500 US Railway Troops who had no military training, 400 from the 2nd Canadian Railway Troops and a ten-gun battery from the 1st Canadian Motor Machine Gun Brigade. As the remnants of the 16th (Irish) Division reached the area, they were assigned to "Carey's Force". They filled a dangerous gap that had opened between the British Fifth and Third Armies, when Bapaume was lost on 24 March.

Everywhere devastation.

The Eighth Day: 28 March

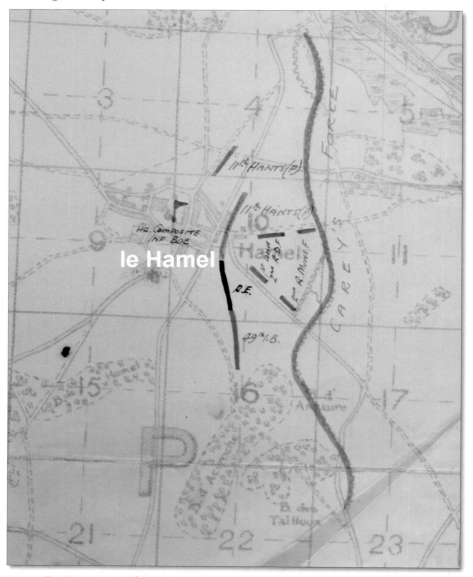

Position of the 48ᵗʰ Brigade on the evening of the 28ᵗʰ March. WO 95/ 1956

The Dublins were now part of Carey's Force. Some soldiers from the 1ˢᵗ Dublins who had become separated were assigned to the 2ⁿᵈ Dublins. This battalion and the 2ⁿᵈ Munsters were placed in support in a sunken road coming out of **le Hamel.**

The 16th (Irish) Division had been reduced to one brigade consisting of four under-strength battalions. Of these, one was a Pioneer and one was an Engineers battalion. They were instructed to counter attack if the enemy got into the frontline. The 45 remaining soldiers of the 1st Dublins left Villers Bretonneux and marched the 3.5 km north to the Divisional Headquarters at **Fouilloy** on the outskirts of Corbie. They were billeted close by at **Aubigny**. Four Dublins were killed in action on 28 March according to the records. It has been possible to gather information about two of them.

Sergeant Joseph Ebbitt (Abbott), MM, 15797, 2nd Dublins

Joseph in 1917 and with his wife Mary Cassell, 1916.

Born in Longwood, County Meath on 21 June 1895, Joseph was the eldest child of Joseph and Mary Abbott (nee Eivers). On leaving school, he worked as an agricultural labourer before joining the Midland Great Western Railway in May 1911 to work as Ballastman at Broadstone Station, Dublin. He joined the 8th Royal Dublin Fusiliers on 4 October 1914 and was promoted to corporal. He married Mary Cassell at St Joseph's, Berkeley Road, Dublin on 5 August 1915. He went to France in December 1915 with the 16th Irish Division and survived the fighting at Hulluch and Ginchy in 1916. He came home on leave around Christmas of that year and returned in December 1917 to visit his wife, parents and seven siblings, the youngest of whom, Patrick, was just eight months old. He remarked that the little fellow would be walking when he saw him again. He survived the first day of the attack and the difficult trek towards safety before being killed in action on 28 March. His body was recovered after the war and interred in Heath Cemetery. He had been awarded the Military Medal on 17 September 1917. He is remembered with others who fell in the Great War on a bronze plaque in Broadstone Station, which is now a bus garage. Christopher Murtagh from Longwood also served with Joseph in the 8thDublins. He was wounded and survived the war to marry Mary Ann, a sister of Joseph, in 1919.*

*This information was provided by Therese Abbott, daughter of Patrick.

Corporal George McCullagh, MM, age 22, 2ⁿᵈ Dublins

Cpl. George McCullagh.

George David McCullagh was from Slieveroe, Stranoodan, Co Monaghan. After attending Campbell College in Belfast from 1910 to July 1914, he worked for the Hong Kong and Shanghai Bank for a short period before joining the Royal West Kent Regiment in London (G/11757). He later served with the 10ᵗʰ Royal Dublin Fusiliers before his final transfer to the 2ⁿᵈ Battalion (26447). His Military Medal had been awarded on 13 March, just two weeks before he was killed. He has no known grave and is commemorated on the Pozieres Memorial. His name is one of five on a memorial plaque which used to be in Cahans Presbyterian Church but is now preserved in the First Ballybay Church.

Major David Nelson of the Royal Field Artillery who won the Victoria Cross for his bravery at Nery in September 1914, came from the same parish. He was killed on 8 April 1918, less than two weeks after George [10].

The Ninth Day: 29ᵗʰ March, Good Friday

Having reached temporary safety, the remnants of the 1ˢᵗ Dublins were incorporated with others to form a force known as the "Aubigny Details". They left for **le Hamel** at 5 a.m. and occupied positions at Bois de Vaire in support of the line in front of Bois des Tailloux.

General Gough and the staff of the Fifth Army headquarters were replaced by Sir Henry Rawlinson and his Fourth Army staff. The Fifth Army was renumbered as the Fourth, leaving the impression that Fifth had been destroyed. Sir Douglas Haig tried to defend Gough by highlighting the lack of troops and the short time available to prepare the poor defences inherited from the French. Gough was not expected to hold his extended line against a strong German attack and had fallen back in accordance with plans. He became a convenient scapegoat to take the spotlight off Lloyd George who had withheld the essential reserves in England. The Prime Minister told the House of Commons that the Army in France was considerably stronger on 1 January 1918 than it had been on 1 January 1917 but he did not disclose that the increase was only in labour, transport and non-combatant personnel including Chinese and South Africans [11]. Gough was ordered to return to England. The promised formal inquiry into his removal was not held. He was never given another command and died in 1963 at the age of ninety-two.

The total number of Royal Dublin Fusiliers who died on this day is 63 according to the Commonwealth War Graves Commission records. This figure appears high in relation to the previous days and the lack of reported fighting. The War Diary of the 2nd Dublins, states that "there was some heavy enemy shelling on the 29th causing several casualties". It is possible that when the records were being completed, a decision was made to allocate the 29th March as a date of death for some of the missing soldiers as this was the last day of the retreat.

It is unlikely that exact records were maintained during the confusion caused by the German advance. The War Diary of the 1st Dublins gives a total of 290 as missing at the end of March. Forty-six of those who died on 29 March have no known grave and are commemorated on the Pozieres Memorial. Eleven are buried in Epehy Wood Cemetery which is close to where the attack began.

Sergeant Andrew Kinsella

Andrew, Mary, and Family, c. 1910.   *Andrew with his wife Mary.*

Among those who are recorded as killed on this day is Sergeant Andrew Kinsella of the 1st Dublins. He was born on 17 September 1882 at 57 Bridgefoot Street, Dublin 8. He had one brother and four sisters. He married Mary Sherry in 1905 in Berkeley Road Church and lived with his family of four sons and one daughter at 33 Arbour Place, off Manor Street.

He was a postman in the Drumcondra area before he enlisted in the 8th Dublins in 1914. He went to France with the 16th (Irish) Division in December 1915. His last child, a daughter, was born in June 1915. He survived the gas attack at Hulluch in April 1916, was wounded at Ginchy in September 1916, and when the 8th and 9th Dublins were eventually disbanded in February 1918, he was transferred to the 1st.

Sergeant Richard O'Brien, unidentified,
Sergeant Andrew Kinsella.

Andrew Kinsella with unidentified friend,
recuperating from wounds c.1916.

His then 12 year-old daughter Cristine recalled how a telegram arrived in the evening and her mother stood up on a chair to read it with the light of the gas lamp. She fainted with the shock when she read that her husband had been killed. The 1st Dublins in the "Aubigny Details" were in front of Bois de Vaire at the time. One of his comrades who survived said that they were near a forest with a river nearby. Andrew was shot by a sniper while using the telephone. He has no known grave and is commemorated on the Pozieres Memorial. His wife survived him by over 40 years. The last of his children, Daniel, died in February, 2007.

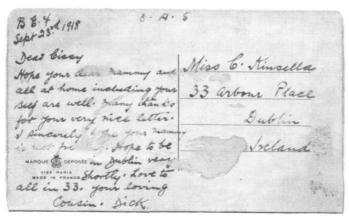

Card sent by Dublin Fusilier Richard O'Brien to Andrew's daughter Cissy.
He was the son of Andrew's brother-in-law. Richard who was a pre-war regular Royal Dublin Dublin,
is shown in the photograph above with Andrew. He survived the war.

The Tenth Day: 30 March

Soon after midday the Germans launched a violent bombardment and attacked from the river to the south of Bois des Tailloux. The Dublins helped to repel this last attack on the former Fifth Army from their position in front of the Bois de Vaire. Heavy shelling by the Germans caused several casualties in the 2nd Dublins which contained some stragglers from the Ist Dublins. Together with the 2nd Munsters, they made a counter-attack and re-took the line, suffering many casualties.

Three of the 2nd Dublins who were killed on this day are buried in Heath Cemetery, Harbonnieres which contains the graves of 1,860 soldiers. Of these, 369 are unidentified. It is possible that some of the Dublins named on the Pozieres Memorial are buried here. For example, the remains of three soldiers buried by the Germans in Morcourt Communal Cemetery were transferred here. One who has a grave is Private Harry Hart. He came from Ditton, Cambridge. His name is on the Memorial Cross in St Andrews Churchyard at Chesterton and on the Chesterton Chapel/Arbury Church War Memorial [12].

The Eleventh Day: 31 March, Easter Sunday

The soldiers of the "Aubigny Details" were reassigned to their own units. The 1st Dublins received 23 soldiers who had been fighting with the 2nd Dublins. At 11 p.m., they relieved the 2nd Dragoon Guards, Queens Bays, in front of le Hamel.

Private Edward Nellis, 1st Dublins, is recorded as being killed in action and has no known grave. The other two deaths on this day were as a result of wounds. The first, Private Joseph Renshaw, from Francis Street in Dublin, died at the Casualty Clearing Station at Namps-au-Val. This is a small village 16 km south west of Amiens, where the Casualty Clearing Stations of the 41st, 50th and 55th Field Ambulance were located during the crucial days of the retreat. On 21 March, they had been close to the Battle Zone but had to quickly transfer their tents, equipment and patients to a more secure area. The 41st CCS, which subsumed the 50th, handled 11,430 wounded men during the month of March, of whom 217 died. [13]

The Namps-au-Val Military cemetery contains the graves of 407 British soldiers who died between 25 March and the 19 April. Among them are two Dublins, Lieutenant Hebron Barrett who died on 27 March and Private Patrick Byrne who died on 30 March. It also contains a grave that is a striking reminder of how ancient military tactics were still in use even at this late stage of the war. Lieutenant Gordon Flowerdew, VC, was killed leading one of the last recorded cavalry charges. An English emigrant, he was serving with Lord Strathcona's Horse in the Canadian Cavalry Brigade on 30 March 1918 when he was sent to push back the Germans at a gap that had developed between the British and French Armies. This was at Moreuil Woods on the River Arve southeast of Amiens and on a main railway supply link to that city.

He led his squadron brandishing their swords in a charge into a group of five infantry companies equipped with machine guns and an artillery battery. Although about 70% of his men were casualties, he led a second attack on the Germans who broke and retreated. Lieutenant Flowerdew was wounded in both legs and died the following day [14]. He was posthumously awarded the Victoria Cross for an act of bravery that had helped to stop the German advance on Amiens. General Ludendorf called off the offensive on 5 April.

Private Ashton Travis died of wounds at the major medical base on the coast at Etaples. His name is recorded on the War memorial in his native village of Blythe Bridge, now a suburb of Stoke-on-Trent. Another soldier from this small village, Sergeant Ernest Egerton, 16th Sherwood Foresters, won a Victoria Cross for his bravery at Passchendaele Ridge on 20 September 1917 when he took 29 prisoners in a solo attack on German dugouts. He died in 1966, aged 66, thirty-eight years after Private Travis [15].

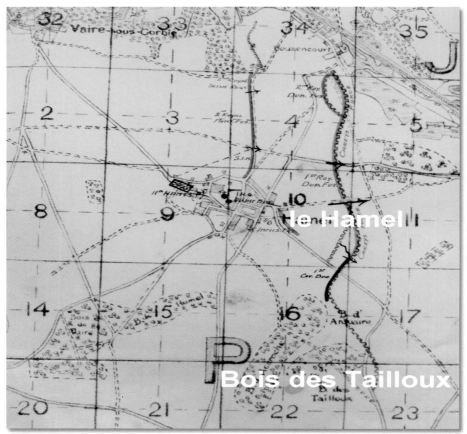

Position of the 48th Infantry Brigade on the morning of the 1st April WO 95/ 1956

A Brief Respite

The two Royal Dublin Fusilier battalions remained in position until the evening of 3 April. The 1st Dublins had received 200 reinforcements. The soldiers marched through **Aubigny** to **Blangy- Tronville**. From there, they were taken by bus to **Saleux.**

The records show that eleven soldiers from the 1st Dublins were killed in action on 3 April. The War Diary does not mention any encounters with the enemy on that day. None of the eleven has a known grave. It is possible that they died from wounds inflicted earlier or perhaps the date was assigned after the event. One of them was nineteen-year old Daniel.O'Dea, the only son of Daniel and Maria O'Dea (nee Daly), of Knockmore, Kilmihil, Co. Clare. He had previously served with the South Irish Horse.

On 4 April, the Dublins entrained and moved north to **Campagne les Boulonnais,** a small rural village about 20 kilometres south west of St Omer, where they arrived on 11 April.

The 5th of April is regarded as the last day of the German offensive in this sector. Twelve soldiers from the 1st Dublins were killed in action on this day. Among them was Private Frederick Smith, aged 18, from Finchley in London. The day before, a Fred Smith was killed while serving with the 2nd East Lancasters.. Two days later, another Fred Smith, aged 21, died while with the 9th Essex. On the opening day of the battle, a Frederick Smith serving with the 1st Dublins was killed in action. All four names are on the Pozieres Memorial.

The Human Cost

By the end of April, the Germans had inflicted more than 236,000 British casualties and captured over 1,000 guns. They had also suffered almost 350,000 casualties who would be very difficult to replace.

**The War Diary of the 1st Dublins for March 1918
provides the following table of casualties:**

	Officers	Other Ranks
Killed in Action	5	40
Died of Wounds	3	6
Wounded	9	253
Missing, believed killed		5
Wounded and missing	7	6
Missing	4	290
Total	28	600

The diary was completed with the best information available at the time. Counted among the missing were about a hundred who were later discovered to have been killed. The 16th (Irish) Division report dated 8 May gives casualty figures of 33 Officers and 800 other ranks. The battalion got additional men during the retreat.

Similarly, the War Diary for the 2nd Dublins gives the following figures for the period 21 to 27 March:

	Officers	Other Ranks
Killed	8	10
Wounded	7	162
Gassed	7	31
Missing	17	713
Total	39	916

The Division report states that 28 Officers and 872 Other Ranks were casualties.

More accurate information had become available by the time the "Soldiers Died" and "Officers Died" lists were compiled. Based on that data, 142 soldiers from the 1st Dublins and 126 from the 2nd Dublins died between 21 March and 5 April. A total of 27 Officers died as well as another 34 soldiers from the other Dublins' battalions. These figures include a small number who died from wounds inflicted in earlier battles. Using the accepted ratio of 3:1, about 1000 were wounded.

The 16th (Irish) Division lost 1085 killed and about 3,255 wounded in the same period. About 1,000 were unwounded prisoners [16]. The Division estimated the total of the Infantry and Pioneers killed, wounded and missing at 277 Officers and 6,672 Other Ranks. In addition, the Divisional Artillery, Engineers and the Machine Gun Battalion lost 55 Officers and 924 Other Ranks. The total casualty figure was 7,149 [17].

The Red Baron

Manfred von Richthofen.

The most famous German fighter pilot of the war, Manfred von Richthofen, was shot down and killed while flying along the Morlancourt Ridge which is visible from the position that the 2nd Dublins had held above le Hamel. He was credited with having shot down 80 planes. On 21 April 1918, he took off from the advance airfield at Cappy and was chasing a British plane when he was hit by a single .303 bullet just after 11a.m. He managed to land his plane on the Bray Corbie Road, just north of Vaux-sur-Somme, before he died. Australian soldiers, who held this area, took charge of his body and organised a funeral with full military honours at Bertangles, near Amiens, four days later. Later, British planes dropped photographs of the funeral over the Cappy airfield with the messsage: "To the German Flying Corps: Rittmeister Baron Manfred von Richthofen was killed in aerial combat on April 21st, 1918. He was buried with full military honours". His body was transferred to Berlin in 1925. Fifty years later, his remains were interred in his family's tomb in Wiesbaden.

Allied soldiers pose with the remains of The Red Baron's plane.

References

(1) WO339/44950 113804/6

(2) *The Blue Cap*, Vol 10, 2004

(3) Correspondence with a relative.

(4) Personal Experiences of the Great War, Frank Laird

(5) Letter from Lieutenant F. M. Laird, 1st [att] 3rd R. Dublin Fusiliers, Weelsby Camp. Grimsby, [Lincs.] to The Adjutant, 3rd R. Dublin Fusiliers, 3 March 1919. Papers of Captain George Evelyn Cowley, soldier, 1810-1938. Co C 25, Nottingham University Library.

(6) Letter from Captain Talbot Considine to A. Cowley, Esq., 22 Palace Road, Streatham Hill, S.W.2. 1 May 1918. Co C 24/4, Nottingham University Library

(7) Irish Times, 30 April 1918

(8) Hogarty, p.142,

(9) Darwen News, 14 August 1920

(10) www.user.dccnet.com/s.brown/biographies/McCullagh_GD.html

(11) Neilands, p.174

(12) www.roll-of-honour.com/Cambridgeshire/ChestertonArbury.html

(13) Byrne, p.110

(14) http://15www.oldframlinghamian.com/images/articles/LIEUTENANTGORDONMURIELFLOWERDE WVC1894-99.pdf

(15) www.egerton.org.uk/

(16) Johnstone, p.389

(17) War Diary of the 6th (Irish) Division. Report on Operations Carried Out by 16th Division. March 25th to April 3rd, 1918. WO 95/1956

Central Advisory Committee Royal Dublin Fusiliers

Dinner and Entertainment

To Welcome the Men of the Regiment who have been Repatriated from German Prison Camps.

On Tuesday Afternoon, 21st January, 1919,

Dinner at the Mansion House, at 12.30 p.m. (by kind permission of the Lord Mayor)
Entertainment at the Theatre Royal, at 2 p.m. (by kind permission of the Directors)

GREETINGS.

HIS EXCELLENCY THE LORD LIEUTENANT, K.P., G.C.B., O.M., G.C.V.O., K.C.M.G.

"I much regret being unable to be present at your gathering on Tuesday. I have deep reason to be for ever grateful to the Royal Dublin Fusiliers for the magnificent gallantry and devotion which they invariably displayed when serving under my Chief Command in the Field. You have my warmest and best wishes.

FRENCH, Viceroy."

H.R.H. THE DUKE OF CONNAUGHT, K.G., Patron, Central Advisory Committee, R.D.F.

"As Colonel-in-Chief of the Royal Dublin Fusiliers, I send my warmest greetings to the Repatriated Prisoners of War of your Regiment who are gathered together at the Mansion House in Dublin; I welcome home these gallant men with the hope that their health will not have suffered by their long and tiring imprisonment in Germany.

ARTHUR, Colonel-in-Chief."

THE RIGHT HON. THE EARL OF MEATH, K.P., H.M.L., President of the Central Advisory Committee.

"As Hon. Colonel of the old 5th Battalion of this Regiment and as H.L.M. for the County and City of Dublin I regret that absence from Ireland will prevent my being present, but I wish to express my sense of regret that I cannot shake by the hand the noble men who have sustained in so world renowned a manner the ancient honour of this distinguished Regiment and have contributed in so large a degree to the glorious Victory of Right over Might. Peace to the Glorious Dead and Honour to the Living Victors!

MEATH."

MAJOR GENERAL COOPER, C.B., Colonel, Royal Dublin Fusiliers.

"Comrades—It is with much regret that I am unable to be present at your 'Welcome Home.' You are all in my thoughts and as your Colonel I wish to express how much I have sympathised and felt for you all in your captivity. May you all spend a very Happy Day and have every good luck.

C. D. COOPER, Major-General."

Programme of the Central Advisory Committee Royal Dublin Fusiliers on Tuesday afternoon the 21st January 1919.

Chapter 6
Aftermath

Aftermath

The failure to break through the British lines did not stop the German offensives. General Ludendorff switched his attention to Flanders where he launched the Lys Offensive on 9 April. This was a scaled down version of the original plan codenamed "George" which was one of the options considered for the opening attack. Now named "Georgette", the attack was directed at the important railway centre at Hazebrouck and the Messines Ridge. After some initial success, this also ground to a halt as did another attempt to sieze Amiens. Three further offensives, Operation Blucher (27 May), Gneisenau (9 June) and Reims (15 July) failed before the Allies struck back on 8 August on what Ludendorff described as the "blackest day of the German Army in the history of this war".

On 14 April, the remains of the two Dublins battalions moved to **Clety**, south of St. Omer. They were amalgamated into a composite battalion of two companies, named the 1st/2nd Royal Dublin Fusiliers. Lieutenant-Colonel K. Weldon, D.S.O., was in charge. On 15 April, this battalion arrived in **Boeseghem**, between Saint Omer and Bethune where it helped to build a defensive line. On 19 April, the 1st Dublins was reformed with 940 other ranks under Lieutenant-Colonel Athelstan Moore, D.S.O. The 2nd Dublins were reduced to a cadre as a Battalion Training Unit with 10 Officers and 43 other ranks.

On 26 April, the 1st Dublins rejoined the 86th Brigade of the 29th Division with which it had fought until October 1917. It was just three years since they had gone into action at V Beach in Gallipoli. The battalion took part in a number of attacks as the Germans were relentlessly driven back. The Commanding Officer, Lieutenant Colonel Athelstan Moore, DSO, was killed by shellfire on 14 October in the successful capture of **Ledeghem**, a village to the north west of **Kortrijk**, Belgium. The British Army had only advanced about 10 km on this front since the end of the Battle of Passchendaele on 6 November 1917. This is in stark contrast with the German achievement in their March offensive. When the truce was declared on 11 November 1918, the Battalion was at **St Genois,** near **Ruddervoorde**, about 7 km south of Kortrijk when the strength of the battalion was 41 Officers and 776 other ranks.

Private Patrick Leaden

Private Patrick Leaden was a plasterer in civilian life with a wife and four children. He enlisted and arrived in France in December 1915. He survived over two years on the Western Front. He came through the March Offensive with the 1st Dublins only to be killed in action on 4 September 1918 in an attack on the German line at Ploegsteert in Belgium. In that attack, 23 of his comrades were killed and 89 wounded.

The 2nd Dublins were transferred to the 31st Division at the end of May. On 6 June, it absorbed the remainder of the 7th Dublins who had arrived from Palestine, having previously served in Gallipoli, Serbia and Macedonia. Most were suffering from malaria contracted in the Struma valley north of Thessaloniki (Salonika). The battalion was given a week to recuperate at Rouxmesnil, near Dieppe, where the men could bathe in the sea. On 15 July, it was transferred to the 149th Brigade of the 50th Division. Further batches of troops arrived during July and August. When it the battalion returned to the frontline in late September, it had a strength of 35 officers and 884 other ranks. They took part in the final assaults on the Hindenburg line along the St. Quentin Canal near **Le Catelet.** This is to the east of Malassise Farm. The Battalion had come through this town during their 1914 retreat. Later, on 17-19 October, the Battalion took part in the successful attack at **Le Cateau** where the Fourth Army took 5,139 prisoners and 60 artillery pieces. The battalion's contribution was 354 prisoners, 9 trench mortars, 37 machine-guns and one complete battery. Sergeant Horace Augustus Curtis, 2nd Dublins, won a VC for his bravery during this attack. The fighting took place near the railway station where the battalion had arrived in August 1914, in the expectation of a short war.

They attacked again on 4 November at the southern end of the Mormal Forest, at **Fontaine-au-Bois**, east of **Landrecies**. Their last action was at **Floursies** where five were killed and 17 wounded. The battalion was near **Dourlers,** north of **Avesnes**, when the war ended.

The End of the 16th Irish Division

During the retreat, the five divisions of General Congreve's VIIth Corps had lost 25,000 men and 135 artillery pieces [1]. The 16th Irish Division had the highest number of casualties of all the divisions involved in the Battle. It suffered 7,149 killed, wounded or missing [2]. It was transferred to XIII Corps of the First Army on 10 April to reorganise and its remaining soldiers were assigned to four infantry battalions and six training staffs. It was used to train American troops at Samer, near Boulogne. It was transferred to England on 14 June and when it came back to France on 27 July, it was composed of five English, one Welsh, two Scottish and one Irish battalion, the 5th Royal Irish Fusiliers. The other Irish battalions were distributed to other divisions. The Division's link with Ireland, as indicated by the Shamrock badge, ceased. John Redmond, who had died on 6 March, was spared the final destruction of his "Irish Brigade".

General Sir William Hickie, writing in 1933, commented that at Armistice, three hundred and fifty Catholic Irish soldiers were serving in a Scottish battalion even though the 16th (Irish) Division had ceased to exist from a lack of recruits.

The Blame Game

A scapegoat had to be found to assuage the political embarrassment of the German success in the early days of the battle. After so many costly failed British and French initiatives, the enemy appeared to have discovered new tactics that could win the war. The removal of General Gough was a clear assignment of blame to himself and his Fifth Army. But there is no doubt that Lloyd George's refusal to allow the fresh reserve troops to leave England was one tangible reason why Gough's lines were so thinly held and the defences incomplete. When challenged in Parliament, he admitted that 355,000 soldiers had been sent across the channel in the month after the attack began [3].

Haig submitted a report on the offensive on 30 July which was not released until October when it was obvious that the Allies were close to victory. Haig made it clear that he was forced to extend his front without any extra troops. He could not provide adequate reserves for the points threatened with the forces at his disposal. He was instructed to adopt the ten battalion divisional structure, even though the German attack was imminent and it would take time for the troops to adjust to the new organisation and relationships. Haig now had 130 fewer battalions at his disposal. He left General Gough with inadequate support in order to have the reserves to secure the Channel ports. The enquiry promised to General Gough, when he was removed, never took place.

On 5 April, the commander of the 16th (Irish) Division, Major General Sir Charles Patrick Amyatt Hull, KCB, felt obliged to write to GHQ, through his superior, to deal with the rumours that his infantry had not fought well during the attack. He most emphatically contradicted this. He pointed out that he had only taken over command in February and must therefore be regarded as unbiased. He stated that the Germans first broke through to his south in the fog and that the garrison in Ronssoy were attacked from their rear. This affected the whole line and led to "bitter fighting". The withdrawal from the Green Line on 23 March was "carried out under difficult conditions in a perfectly orderly manner, units retiring and supporting each other with their fire." On 30 March, they had repelled a determined attack by a fresh German division at le Hamel, inflicting heavy casualties. The Corps Commander had sent his personal congratulations [4].

Most of the Irish soldiers who died in the battle were volunteers. Their reasons for enlisting were as varied as the individuals themselves. The details included in this text show that any general interpretation of their motives would be unreliable. At the national level, the Irish involvement in the war was a logical outcome of the agendas of the two main political parties and Ireland's position in the British Empire. But it was probably simply bad luck that had the two Irish Divisions positioned at the point where the Germans delivered the greatest blow. Some British or French Divisions were going to have to face the expected German offensive.

Reaction in Ireland

The newspapers published reasonably accurate reports on the progress of the battle. Lists of soldiers killed, wounded and captured appeared daily. The official notifications arrived later by post. At the time there were two postal deliveries per day in Dublin. In this age of instant electronic communication, one can imagine the trepidation with which soldiers' families awaited the arrival of the postman or the appearance of a telegram motorcyclist. A year would pass before the missing were officially declared dead.

The opening German successes and the consequential British losses increased the pressure on the Government to impose conscription in Ireland. Sir Arthur Conan Doyle wrote a letter to the editor of The Freeman's Journal, published on 4 April, that was intended to embarrass Irishmen into enlisting:

> *"The world is a strange picture at present. Belgium in slavery, France bleeding from a hundred wounds but still keeping her pale face to the enemy; Britain sending her last man and her last pound to hold the murderer off from his victim; America straining every nerve, with a real fear lest she be too late; and Ireland, fat as butter, wrangling over her parish pump.*
>
> *Has every spark of chivalry gone out of the race? Has she no sense at all of the decency and dignity that at such a time she can hold aloof? If she has an ancient grievance against Britain, she has none surely against Belgium and France. Can she not imagine the disgust which her conduct excites in every free democracy in the world. What are her grievances compared to the terrific world questions with which we are confronted.*
>
> *For God's sake, sir, use your great influence to awaken the people even at this eleventh hour to a sense of their duty or an Irishman will be ashamed of the blood which runs in his veins. If peace comes now, where in the world would Ireland find a friend?"*

He did not seem to be aware that the 1916 Rising had awoken a different sense of duty among many young men in Ireland just as he failed to acknowledge the huge sacrifices already made by the Irish soldiers, most recently in resisting the German March onslaught. Lloyd George's cynical promise of a new Home Rule Bill to accompany the introduction of Conscription found few supporters in a changing Ireland. The newly appointed Bishop of Limerick, Dr. Hallinan, had already refused permission for a Requiem Mass in his cathedral for the repose of the soul of John Redmond.

Lloyd George announced his decision on 9 April and the necessary legislation was passed on 16 April. As well as extending conscription to Ireland:

- The military age was raised form 41 to 50 and in special cases to 55.
- An entire review of all exemption by tribunal.
- Lads of 18 to go abroad.
- A clear out of all men under 25 from Government offices.
- Clergy would come under the act for non-combatant work.

The immediate threat had the effect of uniting the Nationalist Party, Sinn Fein, the Labour Party and the Catholic Church in public opposition to the Government. A meeting was held in the Mansion House in Dublin on 18 April which was attended by the party leaders, including Eamon De Valera and Arthur Griffith. The delegates then went to address the Bishops' meeting at Maynooth. Following this, the Archbishops and Bishops issued a strong statement: "An attempt is being made to force conscription upon Ireland against the will of the Irish people and in defiance of the protests of its leaders. In view especially of the historic relationships between the two countries from the very beginning up to the present moment, we consider that conscription forced in this way upon Ireland is an oppressive and inhuman law which the Irish people have a right to resist by all the means that are consonant with the law of God[5]". The Government backed down. Despite the controversy, about 10,000 Irishmen enlisted between 1 June and 15 October 1918.

While the Kaiser's Battle was in progress, there were indications that the military campaign for Irish independence would continue. On 23 March it was reported that five men accused of illegal drilling in Dublin were sentenced to three months imprisonment. They included Oscar Traynor, Bayview Avenue, and Richard McKee from Finglas Bridge. It was also reported that four rifles were stolen from Eyeries Police Barracks and that a bomb had been thrown in Scarriff, Co. Clare.

Though the war ended on 11 November, the many soldiers captured in the March offensive did not begin to leave the camps in Germany until late December and early January. A special dinner was held in the Mansion House in Dublin on 21 January 1919 to welcome home four hundred Royal Dublin Fusilier prisoners of war. More than five hundred wounded Dublins were brought from various hospitals to take part in the festivities. After the dinner, the men were entertained at a concert in the Theatre Royal. When they left, the Mansion House was used for the first meeting of the Sinn Fein deputies who had been elected in General Election of 1918. This was the first meeting of the First Dail [6].

Some of the veterans returned to their employment with companies such as Guinness, Jacobs, the railways and the banks. A number joined in the fight for Irish independence, notably the former Dublin Fusilier Lieutenant Emmet Dalton, who went on to become a Major General in the Free State Army. A few joined the Auxiliary Division of the Royal Irish Constabulary which was introduced to suppress the IRA.

Lieutenant Francis Farrell, formerly of the 2nd Dublins, was killed while taking part in a police raid in Dublin during March 1921. Captain Christopher Wainright was one of the 17 Auxiliaries killed in the Kilmichael Ambush in November 1920. Some civilian ex-servicemen were murdered by the IRA. John Donoghue, formerly of the 4th Dublins was shot in Ratoath, County Meath on 15 June 1921, and William MacPherson, formerly a Sergeant in the 2nd Dublins, was shot in Mallow on 7 July 1921[7].

Many demobilised men found it hard to find work. The end of the Civil War in Ireland added another 30,000 soldiers from the Irish Army to the labour market. The problems were similar to those experienced in other countries. For example, Thomas Whitham of the Coldstream Guards was awarded the Victory Cross for gallantry when he disabled a German machine gun on the first day of the third Battle of Ypres, on 31 July 1917. In addition, Thomas was presented with a gold watch from the Borough and a clock from the people of Worsthorne, his home village. Having failed to find work, he fell on hard times after the war, and was forced to pawn the watch and medal. Thomas died in Oldham Infirmary in 1924, aged 36. The items remained with the pawnbroker until Burnley Corporation, the former name for Burnley Council, bought them to display at Towneley Hall[8].

The majority attempted to resume normal life in their communities. Like most veterans of the First World War, they did not talk about their experiences. The photograph below is a challenge to a simplistic view of the role of Great War veterans in the new independent state.

Local Band in Tullow, County Carlow, in the 1920s. The banner commemorates the 1798 Rebellion. The man seated at the bottom right was proudly wearing his British First World War medals. The boy third from left, second row, was John Greene, the only son of Michael Greene who was killed on 21 March (Chapter 4).

Commmemoration

The memorial to the fallen of the Fifth Army was erected at Pozieres, near the town of Albert. Panels on the wall contain the names of 14,644 soldiers who were killed in the March Offensive and who have no known grave. Panels 79/80 display the names of 185 Royal Dublin Fusiliers. The cemetery within the walls has the graves of 2,755 soldiers, mainly Australian, who died nearby in the later stages of the Battle of the Somme, 1916. About 50% are unidentified.

This location had no connection with the Fifth Army. Its memorial was originally intended for the St Quentin area but French objections to the amount of land required for British memorials prevented this.

It was in March 1918, that the decision was taken to issue the bronze plaque to the next-of-kin of every soldier who died in the war. It was to be accompanied by a scroll with a suitable inscription.

Not Forgotten

The story of the two battalions of the Royal Dublin Fusilers during the fifteen days of the Kaiser's Battle deals with one event in the four years of the Great War. The personal stories and the background details give some idea of the human cost and the impact on the families involved. The pain did not finish with the war.

The final word on the part played by the Irish soldiers in the battle can be left to Marshal Foch who paid specific tribute to the heroism of the Irish soldiers in a statement issued for Armistice Day, November 1928, ten years after the battle:

"I had occasions to put to the test the valour of the Irishmen serving in France, and whether they were Irishmen from the North or the South, or from one party or the other, they did not fail me. Some of the hardest fighting in the terrible days that followed the last offensive of the Germans fell to the Irishmen, and some of their splendid regiments had to endure ordeals that might have taxed to breaking point the capacity of the finest troops in the world. Never once did the Irish fail me in those terrible days. ......In war, there are times when the necessity for yielding up one's life is the most urgent duty of the moment, and the there were many such moments in our long drawn out struggle. Those Irish heroes gave their lives freely, and in honouring them on Sunday, I hope we shall not allow that our grief to let us forget our pride in the glorious heroism of these men......

I know of no better tribute to Irish valour than that paid after the Armistice by one of the German High Command, whom I had known in happier days. I asked him if he could tell me when he had first noted the declining moral of his own troops, and he replied that it was after the picked troops under his command had had repeated experience of meeting the dauntless Irish troops who opposed them in the last great "push" that was destined to separate the British and French armies, and give the enemy their long sought victory. The Irishmen had endured such constant attacks that it was thought that they must be utterly demoralised, but always they seemed to find new energy with which to assail their assailants and in the end the flower of the German Army withered and faded away as an effective force…..

Again and again when forlorn hopes were necessary to delay the enemy's advance, it was the Irish who were ready for these, and at all times the soldiers of Ireland fought with the rare courage and determination that has always characterised the race on the battlefield [9]."

The phrase "forlorn hope" has changed its everyday meaning since 1928. It was used to describe a body of soldiers selected for some service of uncommon danger or for a desperate enterprise of last resort. "Hope" was a corruption of the Dutch word "heap" meaning a group of men.

The soldiers of the Royal Dublin Fusiliers who endured the opening barrage of the long expected German attack and the survivors who continued to resist against the overwhelming odds, thwarted the last good opportunity of Germany to avoid defeat. The desperate enterprise succeeded.

Notes

(1) *Crown and Company*, p.109

(2) Denman, p.168

(3) *New York Times*, 24 October 1918

(4) War Diary 16th (Irish) Division WO 95/1956

(5) *Irish Times*, 19 April 1918

(6) McCarthy, p.11

(7) O'Corrain, p.3

(8) Final programme of Channel 4's *Not Forgotten* series,11th December, 2007

(9) *Irish Times*, 10 November 1928

Bibliography

Aston, Sir George	*Secret Service*, Faber & Faber Ltd, London, 1930.
BBC	*World War 1: The Great War*, BBC TV Series, 1964.
Byrne, Des	*Memory and Remembrance*, private publication, 2008.
Denman, Terence	*Ireland's Unknown Soldiers, the 16th (Irish) Division in the Great War, 1914-198*, Irish Academic Press, 1992.
Doyle, Arthur C.	*The British Campaign in France and Flanders, January to July 1918*, Hodder and Staughton, 1919.
Hanna, Henry	*The Pals at Suvla Bay*, E. Ponsonby Ltd, Dublin, 1917.
Hogarty, Patrick	*"The Old Toughs" from Milton to Mons and the Western Front 1911-1918: A Brief History of the 2nd Battalion, The Royal Dublin Fusiliers"*, 2001.
Hogarty, Patrick	*"Remembrance", A Brief History of The Blue Caps, The 1st Battalion, The Royal Dublin Fusiliers, 1914-1922"*, 2005.
James, Brig. E. A.	*British Regiments 1914-1918*, Naval and Military Press, 1978.
Jervis, Lt-Col H. S.	*The 2nd Munsters in France*, Gale and Holden, 1922.
Johnstone, Tom	*Orange Green and Khaki*, Gill and MacMillan, 1992.
Junger, Ernst	*Storm of Steel*, Penguin Books, 2004. First published in German, 1920.
McCarthy, Dr. P.	*The 21st of January 1919, an Historic Day, The Blue Cap*, Vol. 9, September, 2002.
Middlebrook, Martin	*The Kaiser's Battle*, Harmondsworth, Penguin, 1983.
Mitchison, K.W.	*Epehy*, Battle Ground Europe Series, Leo Cooper, 1998.
Neillands, Robin	*The Great War Generals on the Western Front 1914-1918*, Magpie Books, 2004.
O'Corrain, Daithi	*The Dead of the Irish Revolution, 1912-1921, The Blue Cap*, Vol.12, December, 2005.
Simkins, Peter	*Major General H.W. Higginson, The Blue Cap*, Vol. 14, December, 2007.
War Diaries:	WO 95/905 19th and 20th Entrenching Battalion.
	WO 95/1879 7th Royal Irish Regiment (Southern Irish Horse).
	WO 95/1956 16th Irish Division.
	WO95/1974 1st and 2nd Royal Dublin Fusiliers.
	WO95/1975 2nd Royal Munster Fusiliers.
Wylly, Col. H. C	Crown and Company, the historical records of the 2nd Battalion, Royal Dublin Fusiliers, Vol. 2, Gale and Polden, 1923.
Wylly, Col. H. C.	Neill's "Blue Caps", 1st Battalion Royal Dublin Fusiliers, Vol.3, Gale and Polden, 1923.

Appendix

Appendix

The Royal Dublin Fusiliers who died on each day of the March Offensive

The following lists contain details of officers and men of the Royal Dublin Fusiliers who are recorded as having died on each day of the attack. The information was compiled from the information in the "Soldiers Died" and "Officers Died" publications, the Commonwealth War Graves Commission records and other published sources. The final column shows the number of the battalion in which the soldier was serving. Many of the soldiers had served previously in other English and Irish Regiments.

In some cases, there is doubt about the exact date of death. This is understandable in the circumstances under which the records were compiled. For example, Percy Bemrose is recorded as having died "between 21/03/1918 and 02/04/1918" in the records of the Commonwealth War Graves Commission whereas the "Soldiers Died" publication gives 21 March 1918. Similarly the date of death of Charles Martin is given as "between 21/03/1918 and 29/03/1918" but "Soldiers Died" gives 29 March 1918.

Most were killed in action but some of the wounded died later in hospitals far from this battleground or as prisoners of war. A few soldiers who died in the period of the Offensive but were clearly not involved have not been included.

The names of those with no known grave are recorded on panels 79, 80 and 94 of the Pozieres Memorial,

21 March Fatalities

Name	Rank	Number	Age	Memorial or Grave	Bn
Abrahams, Frederick. Born in Battersea, Surrey, Tooting, London. Formerly 228873, Royal Army Service Corps. Killed in action	Lance Corporal	40885	-	Pozieres Memorial	2
Addis, Thomas Henry. Son of William Edward and Rachael Addis, of 5 Lebanon Park, Twickenham, Middlesex. Killed in action	Lieut.	-	20	Unicorn Cemetery	2
Ahern, Thomas. Son of Mrs. Mary McDonnell, of Lacken, Blessington, Co. Wicklow. Killed in action	Private	9379	25	Pozieres Memorial	2
Ainsworth, Herbert. Born at Darwen. Killed in action	Private	29798	-	Pozieres Memorial	2
Allen, Matthew. Son of Mrs. Martha Allen, 74 Parson St., Townhead, Glasgow. Born in Dublin. Killed in action	Private	29834	28	Unicorn Cemetery	1

Batwell, George Frederick. Born in Dublin. Son of James and May Batwell, of 6 Almeida Avenue, Kilmainham, Dublin. Killed in action	Sergeant	25207	22	Pozieres Memorial	2
Behan, Thomas. Born in Dublin. Son of Andrew and Mary Behan, 19 Great Longford St., Dublin. Killed in action	Private	19461	21	Pozieres Memorial	2
Belas, Reginald Charles William. Born in Dublin. 49 Newbridge Road, Bath. Killed in action	2/Lieut		33	Unicorn Cemetery	1 (8)
Belford, Thomas B. Born in Suncroft, Co Kildare. Formerly 23465, Yorkshire Regiment Killed in action	Private	40018	-	Heath Cemetery	2
Bemrose, Percy. Born at Wainfleet, Lincoln. Formerly 6997, Lincolnshire Regiment. [Date of death in "Soldiers Died" is 6 April 1918. CWGC gives between 21 March and 2 April.] Killed in action	Lance Corporal	40222	-	Pozieres Memorial	1
Bentley, Herbert James. Born at Wanstead, Essex. Son of William Henry and Martha Bentley, Woodland Avenue, Cambridge Park Rd. Husband of Lily Bentley, 4 Gilbert St., Stratford, London. Formerly 5694, 6th London Rifles. Killed in action	Private	43240	35	Pozieres Memorial	2
Black, Duncan, MM. Born in Glasgow. Enlisted in Dublin. Husband of Ellen Black, 11 Thorncastle St., Ringsend, Dublin. Killed in action	Lance Sergeant	14042	28	Pozieres Memorial He is commemorated on the memorial in St. Matthews Church, Irishtown.	2
Blenkhorn, James Born in Blackburn. Son of Robert W. and Alice Blenkhorn, of 25 Whittaker St., Blackburn. Killed in action	Private	30697	23	Pozieres Memorial	2
Boughey, Frank. Born at Audley, Staffordshire. Killed in action	Lance Corporal	18521	-	Pozieres Memorial	2
Boyle, Charles. Born in Liverpool. Son of Charles and Margaret Boyle; husband of Rosalind Mary Boyle, of 29 Bousfield St., Kirkdale, Liverpool. Killed in action	Sergeant	15468	31	Pozieres Memorial	2
Boyle, John. Born in Clinshea, Co Donegal. Residing in Letterkenny. Killed in action	Private	17857	-	Pozieres Memorial	1
Brady, Daniel. Husband of Josephine Brady, 19 Montville Rd., Fazakerley, Liverpool.	Private	21025	30	Unicorn Cemetery	1

Name	Rank	Number		Memorial	
[Date of death in "Soldiers Died" is 29 March, 1918] Killed in action					
Brake, Percy. Born at Bridgewater, Somerset. Killed in Action	Private	28220	-	Pozieres Memorial	2
Broderick, James. Born at Rathmines, Dublin. Attached to 16th Signal Coy. RE. Killed in action	Lance Corporal	11397	-	Pozieres Memorial	10
Brown, John. Born in Dublin. Killed in action	Sergeant	9585	-	Pozieres Memorial	2
Burridge, Walter Rutland. Born at Camberwell, Middlesex. Son of James and Lucy Burridge, of 84 Clapham Rd., Stockwell, London; husband of Louise Gertrude Burridge, 50 Battersea Rise, Clapham Common, London. Formerly 6199, London Regiment. Killed in action	Private	43190	30	Pozieres Memorial	2
Butler, Christopher. Born in Dublin Killed in action	Private	9385	-	Pozieres Memorial	2
Butler, James, Husband of Florence Butler, of 7 Thomas St., Clonmel, Co. Tipperary. Formerly 2041, S. Irish Horse. Killed in action	Private	27485	-	Pozieres Memorial	2
Byrne, Walter. Born in Dublin Killed in action	Private	24867	-	Pozieres Memorial	2
Cahill, John. Born at Killucan, Co. Westmeath. Residing at Carrick-on-Shannon. Killed in action	Private	28684	-	Pozieres Memorial	2
Callaghan, Eugene, son of Patrick and Nora Callaghan, of Ballyrushon, Castlecor, Co. Cork. Formerly 6394, Royal Munster Fusiliers. Killed in action	Private	40772	29	Pozieres Memorial	1
Camery, Charles J. Born at Marshfield, Monmouthshire. Son of Mrs. A. S. White, of 12 Percy Terrace, Tiverton, Bath. Formerly 7/5517, Training Reserve. Killed in action	Private	41340	-	Ste. Emilie Valley Cemetery	1
Campbell, William. Born at Townhead, Glasgow. Killed in action	Private	17266	-	Pozieres Memorial	2
Clarke, John Thomas. Born at Inchicore, Dublin. Son of James and Mary Anne Clarke, Harbour St., Banagher, Co. Offaly. Killed in action	Lance Corporal	25822	22	Pozieres Memorial	2
Collins, Laurence. Born in Dublin. [Date of death in "Soldiers Died" is 19 July 1918] Killed in action	Private	30321	-	Pozieres Memorial	2

Connelly, Thomas. Born at Hamilton, Scotland. Formerly 3063, Scottish Rifles. Killed in action	Private	20868	-	Templeux-Le-Guerard British Cemetery	2
Cooper, John. Born in Dublin. Son of William and Annie Cooper, of 17 Avoca Square, York Rd., Dun Laoghaire, Co. Dublin. Killed in action	Private	11699	22	Pozieres Memorial	2
Coughlan, James. Born at Cork. Killed in action	Private	27559	-	Pozieres Memorial	2
Crutchley, Frederick, Born Choriton, Staffordshire. Son of Mrs. F. W. Crutchley, The Flosh, Creswell, Stafford. Formerly 22568, North Staffs. Regiment Killed in action	Private	40193	26	Pozieres Memorial	1
Cunningham, Bernard Camelis Josh. Killed in action	Captain		-	Unicorn Cemetery	2
Davis, Francis Wood, M.M. Born at Bedford. Killed in action	Private	27357	-	Pozieres Memorial	2
Deegan, Joseph. Born in Dublin. Enlisted at Sutton. Killed in Action	Private	23233	-	Pozieres Memorial	2
Deegan, Michael J. Born at Ballymore Eustace, Co. Kildare. Formerly 9267, Lancers. Killed in action	Lance Corporal	21601	20	Epehy Wood Farm Cemetery	2
Delahunt, Ralph. Born in Port Louis, Mauritius. Son of Mrs. Mary Delahunt, of 9 Hardwicke Place, Dublin. [Date of death in "Soldiers Died" is 10 April1918] Killed in action	Private	18734	23	Pozieres Memorial	2
Dillon, James. Son of Patrick and Mary Dillon, of 49, Crawford St., Rochdale; husband of Mary Dillon, of Jean St., Wilston, Albion, Brisbane, Australia. Killed in action	Private	17118	31	Pozieres Memorial	2
Dixon, John. Born in Dublin. Killed in action	Private	22371	-	Pozieres Memorial	1
Dolan, Michael Son of Michael and Jane Dolan, 6 Pembroke Cottages, Donnybrook; husband of Annie Dolan, of 14 Beaver Row, Donnybrook, Dublin. Killed in action	Private	25735	25	Pozieres Memorial	2
Donnelly, Michael. Born in Newbridge, Co. Kildare. Killed in action	Lance Corporal	7242	-	Pozieres Memorial	2
Dore, Thomas. Born in Dublin. Son of Mrs. Mary Anne Dore, 31 Upper Gloucester St., Dublin. Killed in action	Private "C" Coy.	27174	20	Pozieres Memorial	2

Doyle, Michael. Born in Carlow. Son of Michael and Annie Doyle, of 5 Burrin Street, Carlow. Killed in action	Private	5602	20	Pozieres Memorial	2
Drain, John. Born at Letterkenny, Co. Donegal. Son of James and Mary Ann Drain, of 2 Ballymacool Terrace, Letterkenny, Killed in action	Private	30327	19	Pozieres Memorial	2
Dryden, Robert, Born at Thomastown, Co. Carlow. Son of Alfred and Mary Dryden, who moved to Field House, Triangle, Halifax. [Date of death in "Soldiers Died" is 24 April1918] Killed in action	Lance Corporal	27215	22	Pozieres Memorial	2
Duff, John. Killed in action	Private	9729	-	Pozieres Memorial	1
Dunne, John, MM Son of Frank and Mary Dunne of Pike St., Thurles, Co. Tipperary. Formerly 11849, R.A.M.C. Killed in action	Private	21859	23	Pozieres Memorial	2
Eccles, Richard Herbert. Son of Christopher and Jane Ann Eccles, 13 Nicholas St., Darwen, Lancs. Enlisted in Barrow. Killed in action	Private	30632	25	Pozieres Memorial	2
Egan, John. Son of Mrs. Catherine Egan, of 7, Middle Gardiner St., Dublin. Killed in action	Private	20220	22	Pozieres Memorial	2
English, Joseph. Moone, Co. Kildare. Enlisted at Grangecon, Co. Wicklow. Killed in action	Private	20335	-	Unicorn Cemetery	2
Evans, Stephen F. Born at Bethnal Green, Middlesex. Son of Frederick and Elizabeth Evans. Husband of Lilian Gertrude Evans, of "Luckham," Stanley Hill, Amersham Common, Amersham, Bucks. Formerly 6601, London Regiment. Killed in action	Lance Corporal "A" Coy	43200	27	Unicorn Cemetery	2
Fegan, Charles. Born in Newry, Co Down Killed in action	Private	17422	-	Pozieres Memorial	1
Fitzgibbon, Patrick. Born in Dublin Killed in action	Private	7245	-	Unicorn Cemetery	2
Fitzpatrick, James. Born in Dublin. Son of James and Catherine Fitzpatrick; husband of Anne Fitzpatrick, of 4 Hudson's Terrace, Bray, Co. Wicklow. Killed in action	Corporal	20184	40	Pozieres Memorial	2
Flynn, Christopher. Born in Dublin	Lance Corporal	19951	-	Pozieres Memorial	1

Killed in action					
Fortune, Edward Born in Dublin Killed in action	Private	23281	-	Pozieres Memorial	1
Fox, William, Bethel. Born in Dublin Killed in action	Coy Sgt Major	10366	-	Pozieres Memorial	2
Gardner, William. Born at Brandon, Durham. Formerly 39984, Durham Light Infantry. Killed in action	Private	41152	-	Pozieres Memorial	2
Gill, Michael Born at Loughrea, Co Galway. Killed in action	Private	24899	-	Pozieres Memorial	1
Glennon, Patrick. Born in Lucan, Co Dublin. Killed in action	Private	19364	-	Unicorn Cemetery	2
Glover, Frank Born at Kilkeevan, Co. Roscommon. Son of Mr. and Mrs. Michael Glover, of Termon, Boyle, Co. Roscommon. Residing at Castlerea. Killed in action	Private	27281	25	Pozieres Memorial	1
Goodwin, William H. Husband of Lillian M. Goodwin, of 49, Crabble Hill, Dover. Secondary Unit Labour Corps, 217th Area Employment Coy. Killed in action	Private	40888	39	Pozieres Memorial	8
Gorman, William Born Bothwell, Lanarkshire. Residing at Uddington. Formerly 13278, Royal Inniskilling Fusiliers. Killed in action	Private	40306	-	Epehy Wood Farm Cemetery	1
Grady Edward. Born at Haslingden, Lancs. Formerly 24929, East Lancs Regt. Killed in action	Corporal	26768	-	Pozieres Memorial	2
Graves, Gordon Born Killdeas, Co. Fermanagh. Killed in action	Sergeant	27012	35	Pozieres Memorial	2
Greene, Michael Born at Tullow, Co. Carlow. Son of John and Elizabeth Greene, of Tullow; husband of Margaret Greene, Bishop St., Tullow, Co. Carlow. Killed in action	Private	18877	43	Unicorn Cemetery	2
Grimes, Thomas Joseph Son of John and Lucy Grimes, of 4 Pleasants Place, Pleasants St., Dublin. Secondary Unit Labour Corps, 217th Coy. Killed in action	Private	8627	33	Pozieres Memorial	--
Groarke, Martin, Born Swinford, Co Mayo Killed in action	Private	26883	-	Pozieres Memorial	1

Halpin, Christopher Born in Dublin Killed in action	Private	9544	-	Pozieres Memorial	2
Harrision, Herbert John Born in Dublin Killed in action	Private	27695	-	Pozieres Memorial	2
Haworth, George Born in Blackburn Killed in action	Private	29823	-	Pozieres Memorial	2
Heenan, Thomas George Grandon Son of William P. and K. M. Heenan, of 42 Derwent Rd., Stoneycroft, Liverpool. "Town Mayor of Lempire", per War Diary report for March 1918. Killed in action	Lieut		23	Pozieres Memorial	1
Hegarty, Thomas James Born in Dublin Killed in action	Private	25962	-	Pozieres Memorial	1
Henderson, James Shipley Son of Mrs. Mary Elizabeth Henderson, of Hay Leazes, Keenley, Allendale, Northumberland. Formerly 2734, South Irish Horse Killed in action	Private	20947	23	Pozieres Memorial	2
Hernon, Edward Born at Banagher, Offaly, Ireland Killed in action	Private	28683	-	Pozieres Memorial	2
Holland, Robert Son of George and Mary Holland; husband of Mary Holland, of 74 Shafto St., Scotswood, Northumberland. Born at Darlington. Killed in action	Private	30470	42	Roye New British Cemetery	2
Holte(n), David, Born in Dublin Killed in action	Private	23702	-	Pozieres Memorial	2
Hughes. John Born at Tallaght, Co Dublin Killed in action	Private	21517	-	Pozieres Memorial	1
Hulbert, James Born at Kingswood, Bristol. Formerly 5561, Training Reserve Killed in action	Private	41389	-	Pozieres Memorial	1
Hutchinson, John Born in Dublin Killed in action	Private	11170	-	Villers-Bretonneux Military Cemetery	1
Jackson, Herbert. (The date of death given on the Commonwealth War Graves Commission record is between the 2nd and 5th March. The Roll of Honour in "Crown and Company" and the "Officers Died" list both show 21 March) Killed in action	2nd Lieut	-	-	Pozieres Memorial	2
Jennison, Henry Son of Mrs. Fannie Chapman, 2	Corporal	18160	28	Pozieres Memorial	1

Greengate, Keighley, Yorks. Killed in action					
Johnston, John William Son of Charles and Annie Johnston, 21 Thistle Lane, Hebburn, Co. Durham. Formerly 39987, Durham Light Infantry Killed in action	Private	41158	20	Pozieres Memorial	1
Johnston, Robert Born at Killargue, Co Leitrim Killed in action	Private	25933	-	Heath Cemetery	1
Jones, Frederick Husband of M. Jones, 34 Upper Mercer St., Dublin. Killed in action	Private	9072	-	Templeux-Le-Guerard British Cemetery	2
Karney, David Noel Son of Joseph Braham Karney and Ellen Anne Karney, 100 Leinster Rd., Rathmines, Dublin Killed in action	Captain, "C" Coy		31	Pozieres Memorial	2
Kavanagh, Patrick Born in Terenure, Dublin Killed in action	CQMS	15567	26	Pozieres Memorial	2
Kennedy, Christopher Born in Dublin Killed in action	Private	18606	-	Caterpillar Valley Cemetery	2
Kirwan, Patrick Born in Clonmel, Co Tipperary Killed in action	Private	25760	20	Pozieres Memorial	2
Kissane, Patrick Born at Ardfert, Co. Kerry. Formerly 7076, Royal Munster Fusiliers Killed in action	Lance Corporal	41464	19	Ste. Emilie Valley Cemetery	2
Larmour, Daniel Born at Shankill, Co. Antrim Killed in action	Private	20423	-	Pozieres Memorial	2
Leveridge, Henry Born in Cork. Enlisted at Shoreditch, London having come from Bangkok Killed in action	Private	20401	-	Pozieres Memorial	2
Loury, Timothy Born in Tipperary Killed in action	Lance Corporal	27487	-	Pozieres Memorial	2
Lucas, Edwin Born at Warmley, Batch. Formerly 5934, Training Reserve Killed in action	Private	41403	-	Pozieres Memorial	1
Lynch, John Enlisted at Dundalk, Co Louth Killed in action	Private	19594	-	Pozieres Memorial	2
Lyons, Francis Son of John Lyons, 17 Werburgh St., Dublin Killed in action	Sergeant	6626	30	Pozieres Memorial	1
Mahoney, Cornelius	Private	20724	41	Pozieres Memorial	2

Born at Brentford, Middlesex. Husband of Mary Ann Mahoney, 103 Douglas Rd., St. Margaret's, Twickenham. Formerly 28679, Royal Fusiliers Killed in action					
Marks, David Born in Leeds, Formerly 149502, Royal Field Artillery Killed in action	Corporal	41016	-	Pozieres Memorial	1
Martin, Charles, born Lusk, Co Dublin. [Date of death in "Soldiers Died" is 29 March. 21 March is more likely given the location of the grave] Killed in action	Private	26380	-	Ste. Emilie Valley Cemetery	1
Masterson, Patrick Born in Naas Killed in action	Private	19636	-	Pozieres Memorial	2
McAuley, John Born in Airdrie, Scotland Killed in action	Private	17282	-	Unicorn Cemetery	2
McBride, John Born in Derryhason, Co Donegal Killed in action	Private	27572	39	Pozieres Memorial	2
McCarthy, Patrick Born in Limerick Killed in action	Private	7030	-	Pozieres Memorial	1
McCluskey, Charles Francis Son of Edward McCluskey, 74 Hill St., East, Glasgow Killed in action	Private, "C" Coy	30377	23	Pozieres Memorial	2
John McEvoy Born in Wicklow Killed in action	Private	25272	-	Pozieres Memorial	2
McGahon, Michael Born at Ardee, Co. Louth. Son of Joseph and Annie McGahon, husband of Mary Ann McGahon, Rathbody, Reaghstown, Ardee. Killed in action	Private	20042	30	Pozieres Memorial	2
McGarry, Patrick, Born in Kincaslagh, Co Donegal Died of wounds	Private	18380	-	Unicorn Cemetery	2
McGrath, Michael Vincent Born in Belturbet, Co Cavan Killed in action	Lance Corporal	27129	-	Pozieres Memorial	2
McGuigan, John Son of H. T. and Mary McGuigan, of Chapel St., Malahide, Co. Dublin. Killed in action	Private	15127	19	Peronne Communal Cemetery Extension	1
McGuiness, John Norman Son of John and Sarah Jane McGuinness, of 39 Malvern St., Newcastle-on-Tyne. Formelrly of the 11th Bn. Attached to 2nd Royal Munster Fusiliers Killed in action	2nd Lieut		23	Pozieres Memorial	-

McGuire, Hugh Born at Birr, Co Offaly. Killed in action	Private	10387	-	Pozieres Memorial	2
McKeever, Francis James Born in Derrygonelly, Co Fermanagh Formerly 2033 Leinster Regiment. Killed in action	Private	22054	-	Pozieres Memorial	1
McMinn, William Born at Thornhill, Dumfriess. Formerly R/4/062741, Royal Army Service Corps Killed in action	Lance Corporal	28208	-	Pozieres Memorial	2
Mehegan, Daniel Joseph. Formerly of the 10th Battalion, attached to the 2nd Royal Munster Fusiliers. Killed in action	2nd Lieut		-	Pozieres Memorial	-
Moore, Michael Born in Dublin. Son of Mary Ann Moore, 20 Lombard Street East, Dublin Killed in action	Private	28071	19	Pozieres Memorial	2
Moran, James Born at Naas. Enlisted in Glasgow. Killed in action	Private	25855	-	Pozieres Memorial	2
Morley, Walter Born at Calne, Wiltshire Killed in action	Coy Sgt Major	10700	-	Pozieres Memorial	2
Moyler, George Born in Thurles, Co Tipperary Son of George and Margaret Moyler, Quarry St., Thurles Formerly 5322, Royal Irish Regiment Killed in action	Private	43034	23	Templeux-Le- Guerard British Cemetery	2
Murphy, Edward Husband of Rose Murphy, Dromiskin, Castlebellingham, Co. Louth. Killed in action	2nd Lieut		28	Pozieres Memorial	1
Murphy, John Born in Dublin Killed in action	Corporal	10346	-	Pozieres Memorial	1
Neill, Charles Born in Enniskerry, Co Wicklow Killed in action	Private	21541	-	Pozieres Memorial	1
O'Brien, John Son of John and Kate O'Brien, Dublin Rd., Naas, Co. Kildare; husband of Mrs. Mary O'Brien, New Row, Naas. Killed in action (Soldiers Died show 25 March as the date of death)	L/Cpl In $8/9^{th}$ Bn	15418	48	Pozieres Memorial	8/9
O'Gorman, Michael Son of John and Annie O'Gorman, 41 Springfield Place, Canton, Cardiff. Died of Wounds.	Private	22880	21	Roye New British Cemetery	1
O'Hanlon, Henry Born in Linwood , Renfrewshire, Scotland	Private	30484	-	Pozieres Memorial	2

Killed in action					
O'Neil, Neil Son of John and Catherine O'Neil, Auchinstarry, Croy; husband of Margaret O'Neil, of 67 Auchinstarry, Croy, Glasgow. Formerly 1051, Royal Munster Fusiliers Killed in action	Private "C" Coy	41196	34	Unicorn Cemetery	2
O'Reilly, Patrick Born in Maynooth, Co Kildare Killed in action	Private	28656	-	Villers Faucon Communal Cemetery Extension	1
O'Rourke, Patrick Son of James and Mary O'Rourke, Drumerheart, Roslea, Co. Fermanagh Killed in action	Private	26506	26	Pozieres Memorial	2
O'Toole, James Born in Dublin Son of Lawrence and Mary O'Toole, York St., Dublin Killed in action	Sergeant	7305	36	Pozieres Memorial	2
O'Toole, John Son of Michael and Sarah O'Toole, North St., Swords, Co. Dublin Killed in action	Lance Corporal	25331	23	Pozieres Memorial	2
Pearce, Albert, Born in Maeynilarth, North Wales, Formerly 15875, Duke of Cornwall's Light Infantry Killed in action	Lance Corporal	24163	-	Pozieres Memorial	2
Pearce, Henry Richard Born in Hammersmith, London Killed in action	Private	18455	-	Pozieres Memorial	2
Pike, John Born in Kilbride, Co Offaly Killed in action	Corporal	21051	-	Pozieres Memorial	2
Prizeman, Frederick Joseph Husband of Mary, 9 McMahon St, SCR, Dublin Killed in action	Private	22801	40	Pozieres Memorial	2
Quigley, Christopher Son of Patrick and Mary Quigley, 73 St. John's Gardens, Islandbridge, Dublin. Killed in action	2nd Lieut		21	Pozieres Memorial	2
Quinlivan, Michael 57 Mary St, Limerick, formerly 7121, Royal Munster Fusiliers Killed in action	Private	40451	24	Pozieres Memorial	1
Reddy, Lawrence Son of Martin and Esther Reddy, Mylerstown, Co. Kildare. Killed in action	Private	24650	25	Pozieres Memorial	2
Reilly, Patrick Born in Tinryland, Co Carlow. Son of Ellen Doyle (formerly Reilly), 79 Leinster St., Athy, Co. Kildare, and the late Thomas Reilly. Killed in action	Private	23163	26	Unicorn Cemetery	2

Reynolds, James. Sligo Killed in action	Private	26065	-	Pozieres Memorial	2
Ridley, Joseph Chilton. Son of the late James and Mary Ann Ridley, 17 Shrift St., North Shields; husband of E. M. Bertram (formerly Ridley), 6 James' Square, Hudson St., North Shields. Killed in action	Private	30682	22	Pozieres Memorial	2
Roberts, William John Son of William and Mary Roberts; husband of Gertrude Eveline Roberts, of "Roedean", Kimmage Rd., Terenure, Co. Dublin. Medaille Militaire (France) Killed in action.	2nd Lieut		26	Pozieres Memorial	1
Robertson, Eric Hume Killed in action	2nd Lieut attd. 48th T.M. Bty.		-	Pozieres Memorial	2
Roche, Joseph. Born Moudlan Town, Co Wexford Killed in action	Private	19236	-	Pozieres Memorial	2
Sander, William Alfred Christopher, MM. Born at Bow, London. Formerly4439. Duke of Cornwall's Light Infantry Killed in action	Private	24040	-	Pozieres Memorial	2
Scanlon, John Francis 74 Clarendon Street, Shirley. Born in Birr, Co Offaly Killed in action	Sergeant "W" Coy	9115	29	Pozieres Memorial	1
Selway, Francis Born in Sidewell, Devon Killed in action.	Private	19440	-	Pozieres Memorial	2
Shelly, Christopher Son of John and Catherine Shelly, 3 Waterford Street, Dublin Killed in action	Corporal	8059	27	Pozieres Memorial	1
Sheridan, Joseph Patrick Born in Dublin Killed in action	Private	30241	-	Pozieres Memorial	2
Smith, Frederick Born in Cahir, Co Tipperary Killed in action	Private	21257	-	Pozieres Memorial	2
Smith, John Ernest Son of John Thomas and Harriett Jane Smith, 36 Hurlbutt Place, Newington Butts; husband of Martha Smith, 53 Webber Row, Waterloo Rd., London. Formerly 6045, 3/6th London Regiment Killed in action	Private	43266	33	Peronne Road Cemetery, Maricourt.	2
Smith, John Thomas Born at Coopen, Northumberland. Killed in action	Private	30548	-	Pozieres Memorial	1
Stanford, Donovan Edward Formerly of the 6th Battalion. Attached to the 2nd Royal Irish Regiment	2nd Lieut		-	Pozieres Memorial	6

Killed in action					
Taite, Frederick Born at Kingstown (Dun Laoghaire), Dublin Killed in action	Private	12903	-	Pozieres Memorial	1
Tallon, Patrick Born at Finglas, Dublin	Private	30046	-	Pozieres Memorial	1
Taylor, Walter. Born in Darwen, Lancashire. Husband of Mrs. H. Taylor, 6 Finch St., Darwen Killed in action	Private	29846	-	Ste. Emilie Valley Cemetery	2
Thompson, George Alfred Brother of Mrs. Mary Jeffers, 39 St Mary's Road, Midldleton, Co Cork. Killed in action	Private	11192	21	Pozieres Memorial	2
Thompson, Nathaniel George Born at Laragh, Co Wicklow Son of Nathaniel and Frances Thompson, Tinahely, Co. Wicklow. Killed in action	Lance Corporal	20199	24	Pozieres Memorial	2
Till, James Leonard Born at Nicholstown, Hants. Son of James and Kate Till, 232 Chamberlayne Rd., Eastleigh, Hants. Killed in action	Sergeant	12882	30	Pozieres Memorial	2
Toohey, Joseph Henry Born in Dublin Killed in action	Private	30175	-	Pozieres Memorial	2
Travers, Francis Born at Kilmarnock, Scotland Killed in action	Private	25264	-	Villers-Bretonneux Military Cemetery	1
Treacy, William Born in Dublin Son of William and Frances Treacy Husband of Susan Treacy, 220 Parnell St., Dublin Killed in action	Private	22861	35	Pozieres Memorial	2
Wall, James Born at Butts, Co Kilkenny Killed in action	Private	18951	-	Pozieres Memorial	2
Warburton, Andrew Born at Chorley, Lancashire Son of John and Annie Warburton, 42 Shuttleworth Rd., Preston; Husband of Elsie Alice Warburton, 14 Russell Place, Great Harwood, Blackburn. Killed in action	Private	29376	38	Pozieres Memorial	1
Ward, Bernard Born in Dublin Killed in action	Corporal	25458	-	Pozieres Memorial	2
Ward, Thomas Joseph. Born in Sligo Son of Peter and Catherine A. Ward, 12 Temple St., Sligo Died of Wounds	L/Cpl	19862	24	Roye New British Cemetery	1
Wheeler, John. (served as Whelan) Born in Dublin	Sergeant	9081	30	Pozieres Memorial	2

Son of James and Mary Ann Wheeler, 8 Arran Quay, Dublin Killed in action					
White, Henry, MM. Born at Newcastle, Kilcoole, Co Wicklow. Killed in Action	Corporal	9980	-	Pozieres Memorial	2

22 March Fatalities

Name	Rank	Number	Age	Memorial or Grave	Bn
Bicker, Bertie. Son of William and Mary Bicker, of Poyntzpass, Co. Armagh. Formerly number 3088 South Irish Horse Killed in Action.	Private	20875	21	Pozieres Memorial	2
Finegan, Patrick. Son of Patrick and Anne Finegan, Drummond, Inniskeen, Co. Monaghan, husband of Bridget Finegan 1 New St., Dundalk. Killed in Action. ["Soldiers Died" shows date of death as 4 April 1918]	Private	30264	29	Ennemain Communbal Cemetery Extension	10
Hayter, Charles John White Son of Mr. J. W. and Ellen Kate Hayter, "Bunbury," Pound Avenue, Burley, Brockenhurst, Hants. Formerly 5849, Training Reserve. Died of Wounds.	Lance Corporal	41382	19	Caudry British Cemetery	1
Hemp, John Son of John and Annie Hemp, Glasthule, Kingstown; husband of Catherine Hemp, 19, Mulgrave Terrace, Kingstown, Co. Dublin. Tailor Killed in Action.	Private	28974	23	Pozieres Memorial	10
Platt, Joseph, Born in Bolton. Formerly 32659 Hussars. Died of Wounds.	Private	28197	20	St. Sever Cemetery Extension, Rouen	1
Redman, Frederick John Born at Holborn, Middlesex, formerly 5971, 3/6th London Regiment. Died of Wounds.	Private	43248	28	Roye New British Cemetery	2
Rossiter, Michael Born Knott, Co. Wexford. Son of Simon Rossiter, 27 Emmett Square, Blackrock, Co. Dublin. Killed in Action.	Private	26672	-	Pozieres Memorial	10
Ryan, Thomas	Private	40029	-	Pozieres Memorial	2

Born at Lieth, Midlothian. Formerly 126255, Royal Field Artillery. Killed in Action.					
Sexton, Terence Born at Laragh, Co. Cavan. Killed in Action.	Private	27095		Pozieres Memorial	1

Private Hayter is buried in Caudry which is 13 km east of Cambrai. This was in German hands at the time. He may have been brought to the German hospital there as a wounded prisoner. Private Platt was buried in Rouen which was a main hospital centre. By coincidence, another Thomas Ryan of the 2nd Dublins died on this day in hospital in Stockport. He was the son of Edmund and Anne Ryan, of Pike St., Thurles, Co. Tipperary and husband of Gainey Anne Ryan, of 144, Grenville St., Edgeley, Stockport. Aged 42, he had twenty-two years Service.

23 March 1918 Casualties

Name	Rank	Number	Age	Memorial or Grave	Bn
Byrne, Patrick. Born in Dublin Killed in Action.	Private	8767	-	Pozieres Memorial	1
Davies, William Henry. Born at Edgbaston. Formerly 13750, 11th (Prince Albert's Own) Hussars. Killed in Action	Coy Sgt Major	28238	-	Pozieres Memorial	8/9
Harrison, Thomas. Born in Dublin, enlisted in Manchester. Killed in Action.	Private	19231	-	Pozieres Memorial	2
Leeburn, Hugh. Born at Glengormley, Co Antrim. Killed in Action	Private	29474	-	Pozieres Memorial	10
Linton, Thomas Edward. Born at Landport, Portsmouth. Died of Wounds.	L/Sergt	10549	-	Pozieres Memorial	2
McCaffrey, J. Son of Patrick and Catherine McCaffrey, of Clonooney, Drummully, Clones, Co. Monaghan. Not recorded in "Soldiers Died"	Private	22049	34	Brie British Cemetery	1
Meir, Francis Edward Born at Golden Hill Stafford. Formerly 10980, Scottish Rifles. Died of Wounds.	Private	21091	-	Tincourt New British Cemetery	1
Nolan, Thomas Son of Patrick Nolan, of Ardristan, Tullow, Co. Carlow.	Private	22297	33	Ennemain Communbal Cemetery Extension	10

Killed in Action						
O'Donnell, Frederick Albert Born at Sligo. Died of Wounds	Private	30491	-	Honnechy British Cemetery	1
Potter, Edwin. Born at Islington, Devon. Son of Mrs. Anna Maria Potter. Formerly 21039, Devonshire Regiment. Killed in Action	Private	40395	37	Pozieres Memorial	1
Smith, Arthur Husband of Nellie Smith, 167 Wood St., Kidderminster, Worcs. Formerly 38191, Hampshire Regiment. Killed in Action	Private	41210	32	Pozieres Memorial	10

24 March Fatalities

Name	Rank		Number	Age	Memorial or Grave	Bn
Brien, Thomas. Born at Bray, County Wicklow. Died of Wounds	Private		19900	–	Rosieres British Cemetery	1
Clarke, George Alexander. Son of Alexander and Margaret Clarke, 68 Whitworth Road, Drumcondra, Dublin. Died of Wounds	Lieut			24	Honnechy British Cemetery	8
Huckle, George Son of Mr G. and Mrs. E. S. Huckle, 19 Eamont St., St. John's Wood, London. Formerly 6679, 7th Bn, London Regiment. Died of Wounds	Corporal		43278	20	Pozieres Memorial	2
Kee, William, MC. Born at Meenagrove, Co Donegal. Died of Wounds.	Captain			–	Pozieres Memorial	1
Rafferty, William. Born in Bundoran, Co. Donegal. Husband of Mary Rafferty, of 9 Underwood Lane, Paisley. Formerly 12442, Royal Scots Fusiliers. Died of Wounds.	Corporal		40056	29	Ribemont Communal Cemetery Extension (Somme)	2

Most of the 55 burials in Rosieres British Cemetery were of soldiers who died on 24 or 25 March. Ribemont is 8 km southwest of Albert.

25 March Fatalities

Name	Rank	Number	Age	Memorial or Grave	Bn
Boulden, Arthur. Born in Putney, Middlesex. Killed in Action.	Lance Corporal	13950	-	Pozieres Memorial	8/9
Cutts, Albert Frederick. Born in Bermingham, Chesterfield. Formerly 1950, Training Reserve. Killed in Action.	Private	40815	-	Pozieres Memorial	8/9
Donovan, Cyril Bernard, MC. Son of the late Fredric and Anastatia Donovan, High St., Hertford. Killed in Action.	Captain		25	Pozieres Memorial	2
Savage, Patrick Leo. Son of Joseph Francis and Mary Ann Savage, St. Albans Lodge, 27 Larkhill, Blackburn, Died of Wounds	Private	27006	29	St Pierre Cemetery, Amiens	10
Shaughnessy, Thomas. Born in Rathangan, Co. Kildare. Killed in Action.	Private	15737	-	Pozieres Memorial	8/9
Wieland, Frederick. Born Widnes. Enlisted at Warrington. Killed in Action.	Lance Corporal	18338	-	Pozieres Memorial	8/9

26 March Fatalities

Name	Rank	Number	Age	Memorial or Grave	Bn
Ascott, A Son of Arthur and Mary Ascott, of Brook St., Ratcliffe, London; husband of Elizabeth Ascott, 10 Ocean St., Stepney, London. Died of Wounds.	Corporal	18871	24	Roisel Communal Cemetery Extension	1
Cahill, Thomas Laurence, MM. Son of John and Catherine Cahill, of Poplar Square, Naas, Co. Kildare. Enlisted in 2nd Bn. Irish Guards, Jan 1915. Wounded Jan, 1916. Gazetted, 1917. Previously with the 8th RDF. Killed in Action.	Second Lieutenant		-	Pozieres Memorial	1
Dunne, Edward. Born at Baldoyle, Dublin. Died of Wounds.	Private	9401	-	St Sever Cemetery Extension, Rouen	2
Humphries, Thomas Francis. Born in Tipperary	Private	40905	20	Etaples Military Cemetery	1

Son of William and Bridget Humphries, Tipperary; husband of Philomena Humphries, of 45 Synge St., Dublin. Formerly 10021, Royal Munster Fusiliers. Died of Wounds.*					
Keppel, John Mercier. Son of John and Caroline Keppel, Graigue Hill House, Carlow Killed in Action	Private	25352	41	Pozieres Memorial	10
Lowe, Joseph. MM. Son of Mr and Mrs F J Lowe, 3 Hollybank Road, Drumcondra. Formerly of the 8th RDF. Killed in Action	Second Lieutenant		-	Pozieres Memorial	1
MacHutchison, William F. Son of John MacHutchison of 5 Orwell Park , Dublin. Formerly of the 7th RDF Killed in Action.	Lieutenant		-	Pozieres Memorial	7
MacNamara, Maccon John. Killed in Action.	Second Lieutenant		-	Pozieres Memorial	2
Murphy, Richard Victor. Son of William Alexander and Sarah Murphy; husband of Alice Mary Murphy. A Civil Servant in the Registry of Titles, Dublin. Formerly of the 7th RDF. Killed in Action.	Sergeant	14200	32	Pozieres Memorial	1
O'Rourke, James Son of Henry and Catherine O'Rourke, of Dublin; husband of Christina O'Rourke, of 82 Parnell St., Dublin. Died of Wounds.	Private	25844	26	Honnechy British Cemetery	1
Sheridan, Leonard. Previously with the 8th RDF. Killed in Action	Captain		-	Pozieres Memorial	2
Whittaker, Leo. MM. Son of James and Teresa Whittaker, 4 Tramway Terrace, Golden Bridge, Inchicore, Dublin. Killed in Action	Company Sergeant Major	9709	36	Pozieres Memorial	8/9
Wright, Ernest Albert. Born in Blackburn. Killed in Action	Private	30589	-	Pozieres Memorial	1

* Part 73 of "Soldiers Died in the Great War" shows Castleconnell as the place of birth for Private Humphries. The data above is from the Commonwealth War Graves Commission.

27 March Fatalities

Name	Rank	Number	Age	Memorial or Grave	Bn
Barrett, Hebron. Son of Robert T. and Jane G. Barrett, Pembroke Park, Dublin. Died of Wounds	Lieut 19th Entrench. Bn., late "C" Coy. 10th Bn.		25	Namps-au-Val British Cemetery	10
Dillon, John. Born in Withington, Manchester. Formerly 16495, Royal Inniskilling Fusiliers. Killed in Action	Private	21913	-	Pozieres Memorial	10
Dinsdale, Albert. Born in Colne, Lancashire. Killed in Action	Private	29362	-	Pozieres Memorial	10
Farrell, James. Son of Charles and Margaret Farrell, of Kilbeggan, Co. Westmeath. Killed in Action	Company Sergeant Major	8694	33	Pozieres Memorial	10
Geoghegan, John. Born in Dublin. Died of Wounds	Private	25830	-	St. Sever Cemetery Extension, Rouen	2
Kenny, Thomas. Born in Dublin. Killed in Action	Private	19693	-	Pozieres Memorial	2
Manning, William. Born in Ardglass, Co Down. Killed in Action	Lance Sergeant	26268	-	Pozieres Memorial	10
McCullagh, James. Born in Darlington, Durham. Formerly 28765, Durham Light Infantry. Killed in Action	Private	20718	-	Pozieres Memorial	10
McGinn, William. Born in Harolds Cross, Dublin. Killed in Action	Private	19817	-	Pozieres Memorial	1
Membury, Bertram John. Son of John and Elizabeth Membury, 100 Middle St., Yeovil, Somerset. Formerly 5157, London Regiment. Killed in Action	Private	43437	36	Pozieres Memorial	10
Palmer, William Samuel Son of Mr and Mrs David Palmer, Tandragee, Co. Armagh. Killed in Action	Lieut		22	Pozieres Memorial	10
Rogers, James Joseph. Born at Fallagher, Sixmilecross, County Tyrone. Killed in Action	2/Lieut		27	Heath Cemetery, Harbonnieres	2
White, Richard.	Private	14815	40	Pozieres Memorial	2

Born in Dublin. Son of William and Julia White. Killed in Action					

28 March Fatalities

Name	Rank	Number	Age	Memorial or Grave	Bn
Ebbitt, Joseph, MM. Born at Longwood, Co Meath. Killed in Action	Sergeant	15797	-	Heath Cemetery, Harbonnieres	2
Delaney, William Son of Richard and Kate Delaney, 40 Usher's Quay, Dublin. Died of Wounds	Private	30795	18	Abbeville, Communal Cemetery Extension	1
Doherty, Neil. Son of Jack Doherty, Claggin, Clonmany, Co. Donegal. Died of Wounds	Private	27327	23	St. Sever Cemetery Extension, Rouen	2
Keane, Patrick Albert. Son of John and Celia Keane (nee Fahy), Moyleen, Loughrea, Co. Galway. Killed in Action	Private	29777	22	Heath Cemetery, Harbonnieres	1
McCullagh, George David, MM. Son of Andrew and Margaret McCullagh, Slieveroe, Stranoodan, Co. Monaghan. Formerly G/11757, Queen's Own (Royal West Kent Regiment). Killed in Action	Corporal	26447	22	Pozieres Memorial	2
McKenna, George. Born in Allen, Co. Kildare. Died of Wounds	Lance Corporal	24614	-	Premont British Cemetery	2
Staunton, Joseph. Born at Dundrum, Co. Dublin. Husband of Mary Staunton, Harbour Cottages, Ballinasloe, Co. Galway. Formerly 6140, Connaught Rangers. Killed in Action	Corporal	40446	40	Pozieres Memorial	1

29 March Fatalities

Name	Rank	Number	Age	Memorial or Grave	Bn
Browne, Frank William. Born at South Walsham, Norwich. Son of James Browne, Keeper's Cottage, Ranworth, Norwich. Formerly 26189, Norfolk Regiment. Killed in Action	Private	40618	19	Ste Emilie Valley Cemetery, Villers Faucon	1

Buck, Thomas. Born in Skibbereen,. Co. Cork. Killed in Action	Private	20124	-	Epehy Wood Farm	1
Buist, Herbert. Born in Eldon, Durham. Son of Robert and Jane Buist, of 52, Albert St, Shildon, Bishop Auckland, Co. Durham. Formerly 35831, Durham Light Infantry. Killed in Action	Private	41043	22	Pozieres Memorial	1
Callaghan, Patrick. Born in Cork. Formerly 10294, Royal Munster Fusiliers. Killed in Action	Private	27946	-	Epehy Wood Farm	1
Campbell, Stephen. Born in Dublin. Killed in Action	Lance Corporal	10171	-	Pozieres Memorial	1
Carson, James Alfred. Son of John and Annie Carson, of 41 Upper Grand Canal St., Dublin. Killed in Action	Private	29864	19	Pozieres Memorial	1
Cloherty, Christopher. Son of Thady and Mary Cloherty, Knock, Inishbofin; husband of Anne Cloherty, Knock. Formerly 7877, Connaught Rangers. Killed in Action	Private	40435	47	Pozieres Memorial	1
Collingbourne, Robert Browning. Son of Henry and Jane Collingbourne, 44 Cardigan Rd., Winton, Bournemouth, Hantsingbourne. Formerly 6500, Training Reserve. Killed in Action	Private	41350	19	Pozieres Memorial	1
Cox, William Waring. Son of John and Ellen Edith Cox, Limerick. Killed in Action	Private	29581	19	Epehy Wood Farm	1
Crowley, William, MM. Born at Rathmines, Dublin. Son of Mrs. Rosanna Crowley; husband of Mary Crowley, 57 Lower Dominick St., Dublin. Killed in Action	Lance Sergeant	15794	30	Pozieres Memorial	1

Dawson, Harvey. Born at Rotterham, Yorkshire. Son of William and Martha Dawson, of 39 Chapel St., Greasborough, Rotherham. Formerly 9863 Training Reserve. Killed in Action	Private	40144	20	Pozieres Memorial	1
Deegan, John Francis. Son of Joseph and Esther J. Deegan, 32 Balfour Rd., Poulton, Wallasey, Cheshire. Formerly 17153, King's Shropshire Light Infantry. Killed in Action	Private	20650	20	Pozieres Memorial	1
Deeming, Harry. Born at Willenhall, Staffordshire. Formerly 17153, Training Reserve. Killed in Action	Private	40970	-	Pozieres Memorial	1
Denton, Cecil Charles. Son of Charles and Maud Denton, 2 Cronbury Rd.,Reading. Formerly 5666 Training Reserve. Killed in Action	Private	41364	19	Pozieres Memorial	1
Doyle, James. Born in Pennsylvannia, USA. Enlisted in Rathvilly, Co Carlow. Killed in Action	Private	29389	-	Epehy Wood Farm. His name is on the Carlow War Memorial in Leighlinbridge.	1
Dunne, Michael. Son of Edward and Margaret Dunne, Nelson St., Athy, Co. Kildare; husband of Annie Maher (formerly Dunne) Henry St., Graiguecullen, Carlow. Killed in Action	Private	5087	28	Pozieres Memorial	1
Eccles, Richard Thomas. Born at Darwen, Lancashire. Enlisted in Barrow. Killed in Action	Private	30765	-	Pozieres Memorial	1
Falk, Nathan. Born in Manchester. Enlisted in Liverpool. Killed in Action	Private	17150	-	Pozieres Memorial	1
Fleming, Thomas. Born at Williamstown, Co Galway. Killed in Action.	Lance Corporal	19830	-	Epehy Wood Farm	1
Ford, Patrick. Enlisted at St. Pancras, London. Killed in Action	Lance Corporal	18015	-	Le Cateau Military Cemetery	1

Friend, John Henry. Born at Stamford, Lincoln. Formerly 13621, Training Reserve. Killed in Action	Private	40146	-	Pozieres Memorial	1
Gordon, Duncan. Born at Benwell, Northumberland. Son of William and Hannah Gordon; husband of Harriet Harbottle (formerly Gordon), 30 Chapel Terrace, Scotswood, Northumberland. Killed in Action	Private	30482	22	Pozieres Memorial	1
Gregory, Charles. Born at Blackburn, Lancashire. Killed in Action	Private	29847	-	Pozieres Memorial	1
Grimes, Patrick. Born at Rathdrum, Co. Wicklow. Killed in Action	Lance Corporal	19576	-	Pozieres Memorial	1
Haddrell, Victor Conrad. Born at Bedminister, Somerset. Eldest son of Samuel S. and Florence Ada Haddrell, 440 Gloucester Rd., Horfield, Bristol. Killed in Action	Private	41378	19	Pozieres Memorial	1
Hall, George Howard. Born at North Shields, Northumberland. Killed in Action	Private	30474	37	Epehy Wood Farm	1
Haynes, Sydney. Born at Camberwell, Middlesex. Brother of Mrs. Lily Bailey, 61 Furley St., Peckham, London. Killed in Action	Lance Corporal	11327	20	Pozieres Memorial	1
Howell, Reuben Harrison. Died of Wounds inflicted on 21March.	Second Lieutenant		-	St. Sever Cemetery, Rouen.	2
Hughes, Joseph. Born in Dublin. Killed in Action	Company Sergeant Major	8981	-	Pozieres Memorial	1
Kiely, Timothy. Son of Patrick and Mary Kiely, Cork Hill, Youghal, Co. Cork. Killed in Action	Private	23295	17	Pozieres Memorial	1
Kinsella, Andrew. Born in Dublin. Husband of Mary Kinsella, 33 Arbour Place, Dublin. Killed in Action	Sergeant	14672	36	Pozieres Memorial	1
Kinsella, Charles. Died of Wounds.	Private	27007	-	Heath Cemetery, Harbonnieres	2
Lewis, John. Born at Dinas, Glamorgan.	Private	25865	-	Pozieres Memorial	

Killed in Action					1
Loney, William. Born at Paisley. Killed in Action	Private	30171	-	Pozieres Memorial	1
Loughlin, John. Born at Naas, Co Kildare. Killed in Action	Private	5739	-	Pozieres Memorial	1
Lynch, Peter. Born in Dublin. Killed in Action	Private	6484		Pozieres Memorial -	1
Maher, Martin, MM. Born at Sterling, Scotland. Killed in Action	Private	17191	-	Pozieres Memorial	1
May, George Henry. Born at Reading. Formerly 5664, Training Reserve. Killed in Action	Private	41409	-	Epehy Wood Farm	1
McEvoy, James. Born at Malahide, Dublin. Killed in Action	Private	9634	-	Pozieres Memorial	1
McGovern, Patrick. Born in Dublin. Killed in Action	Private	11006	-	Pozieres Memorial	1
McInerney, John. Born in Limerick. Enlisted at Hamilton. Killed in Action	Private	28272	21	Pozieres Memorial	1
Morrison, Alexander. Born at Gort, Co. Galway. Killed in Action	Sergeant	10400	-	Pozieres Memorial	1
Neary, Bernard. Born at Kilmacktigue, Co. Sligo. Killed in Action	Private	28046	-	Pozieres Memorial	1
Noon, Hugh. Born at Dundee Killed in Action	Private	39788	-	Epehy Wood Farm	1
O'Brien, John Joseph. Born at Brighton, Sussex. Enlisted at Woolwich. Formerly 33704, Kings Royal Rifles. Killed in Action	Private	20772	-	Pozieres Memorial	1
O'Brien, Timothy. Born in Cork. Enlisted in Cardiff. Son of Michael and Mary O'Brien, 23 Tynypwll Rd., Whitchurch, Cardiff. Killed in Action	Private	30237	29	Epehy Wood Farm	1
Peaston, William. Born at Carualway, Co. Kildare. Son of Walter and Mary Peaston, Weatherfield, Braintree, Essex. Killed in Action	Private	26392	20	Epehy Wood Farm	1
Pender, James. Born at Monasterevan, Co. Kildare. Killed in Action	Private	25543	-	Pozieres Memorial	1
Pritchard, James Albert.	Private	40807	20	Pozieres Memorial	

Born at Old Hill, Staffordshire. Son of James and Hannah Pritchard, 39 John St., Blackheath, Birmingham. Formerly 5943, Training Reserve. Killed in Action					1
Redmond, Patrick. Born in Dublin. Son of Mrs. Margaret Redmond, 3 Bishop St., Dublin. Killed in Action	Private	9982	30	Pozieres Memorial	1
Reid, Robert. Born at Londonderry. Son of James and Sarah Jane Reid, 17 Powerscourt St., Ormeau Rd., Belfast. . Killed in Action	Private	11172	27	Epehy Wood Farm	1
Remon, Alfred Walter. Born at Bethnal Green, Middlesex. Killed in Action	Private	11541	-	Pozieres Memorial	1
Reynolds, Patrick. Born at Cumbernauld, Dunbarton. Killed in Action	Private	13388	-	Pozieres Memorial	1
Ryan, James. Born in Limerick. Enlisted in London. Killed in Action	Private	17675	-	Pozieres Memorial	1
Saunders, Ernest George. Son of Ernest and Elizabeth Saunders, Cann Lane, North Common, Warmley, Gloucestershire. Formerly 5668, Training Reserve. Killed in Action	Private	41434	19	Pozieres Memorial	1
Shannon, Edward. Son of Thomas and Sarah Shannon, Hacketstown, Co. Carlow. Formerly 52047, Royal Garrison Artillery. Killed in Action	Private	20157	27	Pozieres Memorial	1
Smith, William. Son of William and Elizabeth Smith, Lower Hodgestown, Donadea, Co. Kildare. Killed in Action	Private	10254	32	Pozieres Memorial	1
Spedding, Joseph. Born at Newcastle-on-Tyne. Killed in Action	Private	30530	-	Pozieres Memorial	1
Walsh, Charles. Born in Dublin. Killed in Action	Private	19500	-	Pozieres Memorial	1
Ward, Robert John. Born at Ware, Middlesex. Killed in Action	Private	23619	-	Pozieres Memorial	1
Wharton, Joseph. Born at Blackburn. Killed in Action	Private	30444	-	Pozieres Memorial	1

Whitham, Thomas. Son of Thomas and Alice Whitham; husband of Martha Whitham, 23 Thompson St., Padiham, Burnley. Killed in Action	Private	30396	28	Epehy Wood Farm	1
Wilkinson, Jabez. Born in Coventry. Killed in Action	Private	19114	23	Pozieres Memorial	1

Fatalities 30 March

Name	Rank	Number	Age	Memorial or Grave	Bn
Dunphy, Richard. Born in Dublin. Killed in Action	Corporal	6811	-	Heath Cemetery, Harbonnieres	2
Brennan, Joseph. Died of Wounds.	Private	14492	-	St. Souplet British Cemetery. 6 km south of Le Cateau	10
Byrne, Patrick. Husband of Ellen Byrne, 46 Townsend St., Dublin. Died of Wounds.	Private	29934	-	Namps-au-Val Military Cemetery	8/9
Channon, John. Born at Farway, Devon. Formerly 6430, Training Reserve. Died of Wounds	Private	41342	-	Le Cateau Military Cemetery	1
Duffy, Charles. Son of Mrs. Mary Duffy, of 100, George St., Paisley. Killed in Action	Private	29879	24	Heath Cemetery, Harbonnieres	2
Furlong, James. Born at Piercetown, Co. Wexford. Killed in Action	Private	18527	-	Heath Cemetery, Harbonnieres	2
Hart, Harry. Son of Page and Eliza Hart, Fen Ditton, Cambridge. Formerly 27358, Northhampton Regiment. Killed in Action	Private	40253	38	Heath Cemetery, Harbonnieres	1
Hillen, Hugh. Born in Meath, Enlisted in Drogheda, Co.Louth. Died of Wounds	Private	24408	-	Adelaide Cemetery, Villers Bretonneux	2
Howden, Frank William. Son of John and Elizabeth Howden, of Longford. Died of Wounds.	2nd/Lt		24	Wimereux Communal Cemetery	1
McNicol, Robert, MM. Born at Cookstown, Co. Tyrone. Formerly 29639, Royal Garrison Artillery. Killed in Action	Private	21890	-	Pozieres Memorial	1

Pelow, James. Born in Dublin. Son of Samuel and Eliza Pelow; husband of Frances Annie Pelow, 97 Crondall St, Moss Side, Manchester. Killed in Action	Private	24454	36	Pozieres Memorial	1
Welsh, John. Born at Ballymote, Co. Sligo. Killed in Action	Private	26742	-	Pozieres Memorial	2

Fatalities 31 March

Name	Rank	Number	Age	Memorial or Grave	Bn
McNellis, Edward. Born at Ardragh, Co Donegal, enlisted in Glasgow. Foster son of Kate Smyth, of Drumsnad, Ballynahinch, Belfast. Killed in Action	Private	40444	27	Pozieres Memorial	1
Renshaw, Joseph. Son of Mr. W. Renshaw, of 70 Francis St., Dublin. Died of Wounds.	Private	18928	-	Namps-au-Val Military Cemetery	1
Travis, Ashton. Born at Blythe Bridge., Staffordshire. Son of John and Lavina Travis, Exhibition Farm, Forsbrook, Stoke- on-Trent. Formerly 32214, North Staffordshire Regiment. Died of Wounds.	Private	40796	20	Etaples Military Cemetery	2

Fatalities 1 April

Name	Rank	Number	Age	Memorial or Grave	Bn
Gough, Edgar Percy. Born in Wield, Hants.Son of Edgar Henry and Ellen Gough, of Little Snakemoor, Durley, Bishop's Waltham, Hants. Formerly 23473, Hampshire Regiment. Died of Wounds	Lance Corporal	40594	19	St. Sever Cemetery Extension, Rouen	10
Grigson, Walter Ernest. Born in London. Formerly 5854, London Regiment. Died of Wounds.	Sergeant	43400	-	St. Sever Cemetery Extension, Rouen	10
Kerr, Alexander ("C." on Commonwealth War Graves Commission records).	Private	43542	-	Heath Cemetery, Harbonnieres	1

Born N. Leith, Midlothian. Bewton Grange by Dalkeith. Formerly 38080, R.A.M.C. Killed in Action				

Fatalities 2 April

Name	Rank	Number	Age	Memorial or Grave	Bn
Baines, Percy Edward. Born at Peckham, Surrey. Formerly 3774, Army Pay Corps. Died of Wounds	Private	4036	-	St. Sever Cemetery Extension, Rouen	1

Fatalities 3 April

Name	Rank	Number	Age	Memorial or Grave	Bn
Buckle, Frank Son of Mrs. Buckle, 88 Gisburn Rd., Barrowford, Nelson, Lancs; husband of S. A. Buckle, 58 Walton St., Colne, Lancs. Killed in Action	Private	29951	30	Pozieres Memorial	1
Chapman, Robert Ernest. Born at Sicklemore, Bury St. Edmunds. Formerly 1929, Suffolk Yeomanry. Killed in Action	Private	28346	-	Pozieres Memorial	1
Cox, Francis John. Born at West Bromwich, Staffordshire. Formerly 5968, Training Reserve. Killed in Action	Private	40799	-	Pozieres Memorial	1
Ennis, John. Born in Ranelagh, Dublin. Killed in Action	Private	26387	36	Pozieres Memorial	1
Hickman, Alfred Ernest. Born at Andover, Hampshire. Formerly 6491, Training Battalion. Died of Wounds	Private	41385	-	St. Sever Cemetery Extension, Rouen	1
Hill, George Hewitt. Born at Burnley. Enlisted at Barrow-on-Furness. Died of Wounds	Private	29981	-	Valenciennes(St.Roch) Communal Cemetery	2
Moran, Patrick Born at Carlow. Killed in Action	Private	9502	-	Pozieres Memorial	1
O'Dea, Daniel. Only son of Daniel and Maria	Private	20961	19	Pozieres Memorial	1

Contents

Introduction

Welcome to Carbs & Cals. This is a unique book, the likes of which has not been seen before. Unlike most books, there are lots of pictures and few words.

This book has been produced with two main purposes in mind; first and foremost it provides a fantastic resource for anyone with diabetes who is carbohydrate counting or thinking of learning to carb count. Secondly, for anyone who is trying to lose weight by counting calories or needs advice on portion control, it is a great visual reference to hundreds of different food items and drinks. For the first time, it gives you the ability to see photos of the portions you could choose, and how many calories you could save by making reductions in portion sizes or choosing lower calorie alternatives.

As this is primarily a carbohydrate counting book, foods with no or minimal carbohydrate content have not been included. These include meat, fish, eggs, cheese, oils & spreads, and some vegetables. We have included a large selection of popular food items, meals and drinks.

We hope you enjoy the book and that it makes the process of carbohydrate counting easier to understand.

What is carbohydrate?

Within our diets we have three main food groups. These are fat, protein and carbohydrate.

Carbohydrate foods provide the body with its main energy source, which is glucose. Carbohydrate is broken down by the body into glucose, which is then taken into our blood stream. The rate at which this happens depends on the type of carbohydrate eaten; this is known as the glycaemic index (GI). For example, white bread is readily broken down and causes a quick increase in blood glucose, whereas pasta is more slowly broken down, giving a more gradual increase.

For people contolling their diabetes with insulin, it is useful to have an understanding of the speed at which blood glucose may rise after certain meals or snacks. This can help you to predict your blood glucose level after eating or drinking. If you are adjusting insulin, speak to your diabetes team about this in more detail.

One of the main drawbacks of GI is that it does not take into account the other nutrients in the meal (e.g. protein and fat content), which can slow the absorption of glucose into the blood stream. It also fails to take into account the amount of carbohydrate in the meal, which is a much better predictor of blood glucose response. For people with diabetes, it is therefore important that they have an understanding of the total carbohydrate content of the food and drink they are consuming.

The table on the opposite page shows the main types of food that we eat that contain carbohydrate.

Food Group	Examples	Function
Starchy Foods	Bread, potato, rice, pasta, noodles, breakfast cereal, pastry, yam, cassava, pulses and grains e.g. cous cous	Provides fibre within the diet, especially wholegrain varieties. Also an important source of calcium, iron and B vitamins
Fruit & Vegetables	All types of fruit contain natural fruit sugar (fructose). Vegetables vary in the amount of carbohydrate they contain. Parsnips, butternut squash and other root vegetables generally contain higher amounts of carbs	A great source of vitamins, minerals and fibre within the diet
Dairy Foods	Milk, yoghurt, custard and ice cream all contain milk sugar (lactose)	Provides an important source of calcium, vitamins A and B12. Also contains a good source of protein
Sugary Foods	Sugar, jam, marmalade, honey, soft drinks, sweets, cakes, biscuits and chocolates	No nutritional benefits other than providing an energy source to the body

How much carbohydrate should I eat each day?

The amount of carbohydrate we should eat in a day varies from person to person depending on your activity levels, gender, age and weight. It is estimated that we should get around 50% of our energy from carbohydrate sources. No more than 35% should come from fat and around 10-20% should be from protein.

Within our diets, we have 5 main food groups. The Eatwell Plate shows how much of what you eat should come from each food group. This includes everything you eat during the day, including snacks. Try to eat plenty of fruit and vegetables, plenty of bread, rice, potatoes, pasta and other starchy foods (choose wholegrain varieties whenever you can), some milk and dairy foods, some meat, fish, eggs, beans and other non-dairy sources of protein, and just a small amount of food and drinks that are high in fat and/or sugar.

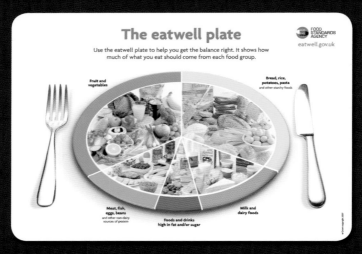

For people with diabetes, the current recommendation (from 2003), is that carbohydrate should make up 45-60% of energy intake. Diabetes UK is currently reviewing this recommendation and it is possible that scientific evidence may result in this value being amended in the future.

The table below shows the amount of carbohydrate per day for different calorie intakes based on 50% of energy:

Calories	Carbohydrate per day (based on 50% of calories)
1500 kcal	190g
2000 kcal	250g
2500 kcal	315g
3000 kcal	375g

Diabetes and Carbohydrate Counting

Carbohydrate counting for people with diabetes is not a new concept; it has been around for over 50 years. However, in recent years it has been incorporated more and more into the education and management of Type 1, Type 2 and diabetes in pregnancy.

Carbohydrate counting means being able to estimate the amount of carbohydrate in a meal, drink or snack by various means (e.g. estimating by sight, looking at food labels or weighing food items).

If you are starting out with carbohydrate counting, there are three main steps to consider:

1. Basic introduction to the concept of carbohydrate counting and understanding the amount of carbohydrate in the diet.

2. Understanding the relationships between food, diabetes medications, physical activity, and blood glucose level, and introducing the steps needed to manage these factors.

3. If you have Type 1 diabetes (and are using multiple daily injections or an insulin pump), learning how to match quick-acting insulin to carbohydrate, using carbohydrate-to-insulin ratios.

Learning to estimate the amount of carbohydrate can be hard work and very time-consuming; even experts in the field of diabetes can have difficulty in calculating carbohydrate. Eating out, take-away meals and dinner with friends can be especially challenging, as it is difficult to know what ingredients have been used and you may be eating foods you are not used to.

When we eat carbohydrate, whether it is pasta, bread, potato, fruit, milk or sugar, it is broken down in our stomachs into glucose. This glucose is then transferred into the blood stream and from there it is carried into cells of the body by the hormone insulin. The amount of insulin required is directly related to the total amount of carbohydrate in the meal or snack being eaten.

It is important to note that certain foods which are broken down into glucose very slowly may not require insulin or may require a reduced dose. This includes foods such as pearl barley, peas, beans and lentils, some vegetables including sweetcorn, squash/pumpkin and parsnips, and some fruit including cherries and grapefruit. It is important that you speak with your diabetes team about whether you may need to take insulin for these foods as it varies from person to person.

Due to the development of newer, quick-acting insulin such as Novorapid, Humalog and Apidra, adjusting the dose of insulin to the specific amount of carbohydrate in a meal has become possible. By adjusting insulin it is possible to have greater flexibility of food choice, reduced risk of hypoglycaemia and improved blood glucose control.

For people on multiple daily injections of insulin (basal bolus) or insulin pumps, knowing the amount of carbohydrate is important to make decisions about the amount of insulin to use. Many people on two injections a day find it useful to count carbohydrate in order to keep to similar amounts at each meal time.

In the UK, people with diabetes who are learning about carbohydrate counting are usually taught to take an amount of insulin based on each 10g of carbohydrate they eat. For example, many people are started on 1 unit of quick-acting insulin for every 10g of carbohydrate they consume. However, some people may need as much as 3 units or more per 10g of carbs. This rate will vary from person to person and can also vary at different times of the day. Your diabetes team can help to advise you on this. Please consult your diabetes centre if you require more information.

Learning how to adjust insulin and count carbohydrate can be complex. This book is not designed to teach you how to adjust your insulin regimen; it is important that you have the support of an appropriately trained health care professional such as a diabetes specialist nurse and dietitian.

Many areas of the UK now offer structured education courses such as BERTIE and DAFNE for Type 1 diabetes, and X-PERT and DESMOND for Type 2 diabetes. These courses can give a much greater insight into carbohydrate counting, as well as self-management of diabetes.

Diabetes and alcohol

Within this book, values have been included for alcoholic drinks that contain carbohydrate. These have been included as a reference only. Extreme caution should be taken when giving additional units of insulin with alcohol as you are more prone to hypoglycaemia (low blood glucose). Speak to your diabetes team about this in more detail.

What are calories?

Calories are units of energy. They are used to measure the amount of energy in the food and drink that we consume. This energy comes from the nutrients carbohydrate, fat, protein and alcohol.

Each of these nutrients contain a different number of calories per gram:

> 1g Carbohydrate = 4 kcal
> 1g Fat = 9 kcal
> 1g Protein = 4 kcal
> 1g Alcohol = 7 kcal

As seen above, fat has the most calories per gram. This is why if you eat a lot of foods that are high in fat, you will consume more calories and are likely to gain more weight.

People often associate carbohydrate with being 'fattening'. However as you can see above, carbohydrate contains the same calories per gram as protein. It is often the way people prepare the carbohydrate food (e.g. adding extra fat to a jacket potato, or frying) that increases the calorie content.

How many calories should I eat each day?

The amount of calories a person should eat or drink depends on a number of different factors. These include age, gender, physical activity levels and whether or not you are trying to lose, maintain or gain weight.

The guideline daily amount (GDA) of calories for a female is 2000, and 2500 for men. These figures are based on an average person. Sometimes GDAs are labelled 'for adults' - these figures are based on the GDA for women to encourage people who need less energy to consume fewer calories. People who are very active, overweight, or obese will have greater calorie requirements to maintain their current weight. It is possible to get a more accurate idea of your calorie needs per day by speaking to a registered dietitian.

Why count calories?

If you are trying to lose weight, it is useful to have an understanding of the calories contained in the food and drink you consume. It is also useful to have a realistic expectation of how many calories to cut down on and what weight loss you should expect.

Studies have shown that in order to lose 1lb of body weight over the course of a week, you need to reduce calories by around 500 per day (3500 per week). This reduction could be by diet alone, or by a combination of diet and increased physical activity. 500 calories is a large reduction, therefore it may be more beneficial to look at a 100-200 calorie reduction to start with.

By eating a slightly smaller portion, or going for a healthier snack, this should be more achievable. See below for an example of how you could save 336 calories by choosing a healthier snack option:

Chocolate Muffin		Strawberries	
55g CARBS	404 CALS	15g CARBS	68 CALS
Weight: 105g		Weight: 250g	

Advice on losing weight

Although the primary focus of this book is to look at carbohydrate counting, each picture also displays the calorie content. This provides a useful tool to track how many calories you are consuming in every meal or snack.

If you are trying to lose weight it is important to follow a balanced diet, including foods from all groups. You may wish to speak to a health care professional such as your GP, practice nurse or dietitian. If you have diabetes and take diabetes medication and/or insulin, weight loss may require a change in medication; it is best to seek medical advice first.

The British Dietetic Association (BDA) has developed a website (www.bdaweightwise.com) containing lots of useful hints and tips on losing weight. Diabetes UK (www.diabetes.org.uk) also has advice on weight loss, shopping tips and recipe ideas.

How to use this book

Carbs & Cals has been written with complete practicality in mind. The process of using the book is as follows:

1. Prepare your meal, drink or snack as normal.
2. Find the meal, drink or snack in the book.
3. Choose the portion photo that is closest to your own.
4. If you are carb counting, use the value in green above that photo, and if you are calorie counting, use the value in blue above that photo.
5. Add up the carb or calorie values for the different food components to give the totals for your meal.

All foods are displayed on one of the following dishes:

26cm Dinner Plate

20cm Side Plate

22cm Large Bowl

14cm Cereal Bowl

Each picture displays either a knife & fork, or a dessert spoon to help with scale. It may be a good idea to measure your own crockery to see how the size of your plates and bowls compares with the ones in the pictures, and possibly choose plates and bowls of a similar size to the ones shown to make it as easy as possible.

Foods are arranged in logical, alphabetical sections of Biscuits & Crackers, Bread, Breakfast, Cakes & Bakery Items, Desserts, Drinks, Fruit, Meals, Meal Accompaniments, Meat & Fish, Potatoes, Rice, Pasta & Grains, Snacks, Take-aways, and Vegetables & Pulses. The different sections are coloured so it's easy to find the food or drink you are looking for.

If you are eating a meal with multiple carbohydrate components (e.g. roast dinner, or cooked breakfast), you will need to find the various components in the book and add them up separately. For example, your roast dinner may comprise of Yorkshire puddings from page 152, stuffing from page 152, roast potatoes from page 171, parsnips from page 231, and cranberry sauce from page 153.

Each food has between 1 and 6 portion examples, so you can easily judge the carbs and cals in your particular portion just by looking at the different photos. For example, a digestive biscuit is always the same size, so only 1 photo has been included. However, there are 6 different portion pictures of lasagne included so that you can choose the portion that is closest to the portion on your plate.

The carb value is always in a large green tab, and the calorie value is in a large blue tab, so it's easy to see the values you are looking for.

50g CARBS   **326** CALS

The weight of each portion is stated underneath each photo, just in case you want to double-check the weight of your own portion. **This is always the cooked / prepared weight.**

Weight: 170g

For foods that you are likely to have several of, there is a table with the carbs and cals for 1, 2, 3 and 4 pieces, to make it even easier for you to add up.

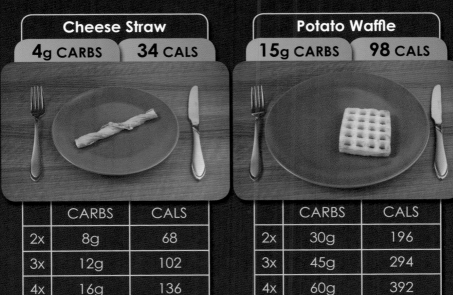

Cheese Straw		
4g CARBS	**34** CALS	
	CARBS	CALS
2x	8g	68
3x	12g	102
4x	16g	136
Weight: 7g		

Potato Waffle		
15g CARBS	**98** CALS	
	CARBS	CALS
2x	30g	196
3x	45g	294
4x	60g	392
Weight: 49g		

Bourbon Cream

8g CARBS   **59 CALS**

	CARBS	CALS
2x	16g	118
3x	24g	177
4x	32g	236
Weight: 12g	

Chocolate Digestive

9g CARBS   **73 CALS**

	CARBS	CALS
2x	18g	146
3x	27g	219
4x	36g	292
Weight: 15g	

Chocolate Chip Cookie

7g CARBS   **47 CALS**

	CARBS	CALS
2x	14g	94
3x	21g	141
4x	28g	188
Weight: 10g	

48g CARBS   **351 CALS**

	CARBS	CALS
2x	96g	702
3x	144g	1053
4x	192g	1404
Weight: 74g	

Chocolate Oat Biscuit

13g CARBS   **100 CALS**

	CARBS	CALS
2x	26g	200
3x	39g	300
4x	52g	400
Weight: 19g		

Custard Cream

8g CARBS   **58 CALS**

	CARBS	CALS
2x	16g	116
3x	24g	174
4x	32g	232
Weight: 12g		

Digestive

10g CARBS   **71 CALS**

	CARBS	CALS
2x	20g	142
3x	30g	213
4x	40g	284
Weight: 15g		

Fig Roll

15g CARBS   **80 CALS**

	CARBS	CALS
2x	30g	160
3x	45g	240
4x	60g	320
Weight: 21g		

Ginger Biscuit

8g CARBS   **44 CALS**

	CARBS	CALS
2x	16g	88
3x	24g	132
4x	32g	176
Weight: 10g		

Gingerbread Man

38g CARBS   **220 CALS**

	CARBS	CALS
2x	76g	440
3x	114g	660
4x	152g	880
Weight: 58g		

Iced Ring

5g CARBS   **27 CALS**

	CARBS	CALS
2x	10g	54
3x	15g	81
4x	20g	108
Weight: 6g		

Jaffa Cake

9g CARBS   **47 CALS**

	CARBS	CALS
2x	18g	94
3x	27g	141
4x	36g	188
Weight: 13g		

Jam Ring

13g CARBS | **79** CALS

	CARBS	CALS
2x	26g	158
3x	39g	237
4x	52g	316
Weight: 18g		

Malted Milk

5g CARBS | **39** CALS

	CARBS	CALS
2x	10g	78
3x	15g	117
4x	20g	156
Weight: 8g		

Nice

5g CARBS | **39** CALS

	CARBS	CALS
2x	10g	78
3x	15g	117
4x	20g	156
Weight: 8g		

Oat Biscuit

10g CARBS | **75** CALS

	CARBS	CALS
2x	20g	150
3x	30g	225
4x	40g	300
Weight: 16g		

Pink Wafer

| 6g CARBS | 48 CALS |

	CARBS	CALS
2x	12g	96
3x	18g	144
4x	24g	192
Weight: 9g		

Rich Tea

| 5g CARBS | 33 CALS |

	CARBS	CALS
2x	10g	66
3x	15g	99
4x	20g	132
Weight: 7g		

Shortbread Finger

| 10g CARBS | 80 CALS |

	CARBS	CALS
2x	20g	160
3x	30g	240
4x	40g	320
Weight: 16g		

Shortcake

| 7g CARBS | 49 CALS |

	CARBS	CALS
2x	14g	98
3x	21g	147
4x	28g	196
Weight: 10g		

Breadstick

4g CARBS	**21** CALS

	CARBS	CALS
2x	8g	42
3x	12g	63
4x	16g	84
Weight: 5g		

Cheddar

2g CARBS	**27** CALS

	CARBS	CALS
2x	4g	54
3x	6g	81
4x	8g	108
Weight: 5g		

Cheese Straw

4g CARBS	**34** CALS

	CARBS	CALS
2x	8g	68
3x	12g	102
4x	16g	136
Weight: 7g		

Cream Cracker

5g CARBS	**35** CALS

	CARBS	CALS
2x	10g	70
3x	15g	105
4x	20g	140
Weight: 8g		

Crispbread (thin)

4g CARBS   **19 CALS**

	CARBS	CALS
2x	8g	38
3x	12g	57
4x	16g	76
Weight: 6g		

Crispbread

8g CARBS   **35 CALS**

	CARBS	CALS
2x	16g	70
3x	24g	105
4x	32g	140
Weight: 11g		

Digestive (savoury)

9g CARBS   **85 CALS**

	CARBS	CALS
2x	18g	170
3x	27g	255
4x	36g	340
Weight: 13g		

Oatcake

6g CARBS   **44 CALS**

	CARBS	CALS
2x	12g	88
3x	18g	132
4x	24g	176
Weight: 10g		

Puffed Cracker

5g CARBS   **48** CALS

	CARBS	CALS
2x	10g	96
3x	15g	144
4x	20g	192
Weight: 9g		

Rice Cake

6g CARBS   **30** CALS

	CARBS	CALS
2x	12g	60
3x	18g	90
4x	24g	120
Weight: 8g		

Water Biscuit

4g CARBS   **24** CALS

	CARBS	CALS
2x	8g	48
3x	12g	72
4x	16g	96
Weight: 6g		

Wholegrain Cracker

5g CARBS   **34** CALS

	CARBS	CALS
2x	10g	68
3x	15g	102
4x	20g	136
Weight: 8g		

Sliced Bread (granary)

5g CARBS	26 CALS

Weight: 11g (thin slice)

10g CARBS	52 CALS

Weight: 22g (thin slice)

15g CARBS	78 CALS

Weight: 33g (medium slice)

20g CARBS	103 CALS

Weight: 44g (thick slice)

30g CARBS	150 CALS

Weight: 64g (extra thick slice)

40g CARBS	202 CALS

Weight: 86g

Sliced Bread (white)

5g CARBS   **24 CALS**

Weight: 11g (thin slice)

10g CARBS   **48 CALS**

Weight: 22g (thin slice)

15g CARBS   **72 CALS**

Weight: 33g (medium slice)

20g CARBS   **93 CALS**

Weight: 43g (thick slice)

30g CARBS   **139 CALS**

Weight: 64g (extra thick slice)

40g CARBS   **184 CALS**

Weight: 85g

Sliced Bread (wholemeal)

5g CARBS **24** CALS	**10**g CARBS **49** CALS

Weight: 11g (thin slice)	Weight: 23g (thin slice)

15g CARBS **77** CALS	**20**g CARBS **105** CALS

Weight: 36g (medium slice)	Weight: 49g (thick slice)

30g CARBS **153** CALS	**40**g CARBS **204** CALS

Weight: 71g (extra thick slice)	Weight: 95g

Bap (white)

25g CARBS   **124 CALS**   **60g CARBS**   **299 CALS**

Weight: 48g   Weight: 116g

Bap (wholemeal)

25g CARBS   **123 CALS**   **55g CARBS**   **275 CALS**

Weight: 51g   Weight: 114g

Crusty Roll (white)

25g CARBS   **120 CALS**   **50g CARBS**   **241 CALS**

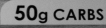

Weight: 43g   Weight: 86g

Bagel

50g CARBS   **235** CALS

Weight: 86g

Burger Bun

40g CARBS   **216** CALS

Weight: 82g

Finger Roll

20g CARBS   **105** CALS

Weight: 41g

Poppy Seeded Roll

30g CARBS   **149** CALS

Weight: 54g

Pitta Bread

40g CARBS   **183** CALS

Weight: 69g

Pitta Bread (mini)

20g CARBS   **93** CALS

Weight: 35g

Ciabatta

50g CARBS | **263 CALS**

Weight: 97g

Panini

45g CARBS | **272 CALS**

Weight: 100g

French Stick (slice)

20g CARBS | **100 CALS**

Weight: 37g

French Stick (small)

65g CARBS | **319 CALS**

Weight: 118g

Garlic Bread

10g CARBS | **80 CALS**

Weight: 22g

30g CARBS | **241 CALS**

Weight: 66g

Crumpet

20g CARBS	90 CALS

Weight: 45g

Crumpet (square)

25g CARBS	113 CALS

Weight: 57g

English Muffin

30g CARBS	152 CALS

Weight: 68g

Tea Cake

50g CARBS	280 CALS

Weight: 85g

Tortilla

35g CARBS	152 CALS

Weight: 58g

Turkish Flatbread

30g CARBS	157 CALS

Weight: 60g

Naan Bread

70g CARBS | **470 CALS**

Weight: 140g

Naan Bread (mini)

30g CARBS | **202 CALS**

Weight: 60g

Chapati

20g CARBS | **91 CALS**

Weight: 45g

Paratha

40g CARBS | **297 CALS**

Weight: 92g

Poppadom (small)

5g CARBS | **48 CALS**

Weight: 13g

Poppadom (large)

10g CARBS | **92 CALS**

Weight: 25g

Brioche

| 10g CARBS | 62 CALS | 25g CARBS | 156 CALS |

Weight: 18g

Weight: 45g

Croissant

| 10g CARBS | 94 CALS | 20g CARBS | 184 CALS |

Weight: 26g

Weight: 51g

Pain au Chocolat

| 15g CARBS | 134 CALS | 30g CARBS | 269 CALS |

Weight: 32g

Weight: 64g

Toast with Chocolate Spread

8g CARBS   **65 CALS**

	CARBS	CALS
2x	16g	130
3x	24g	195
4x	32g	260
Weight: 13g (medium slice)		

15g CARBS   **128 CALS**

	CARBS	CALS
2x	30g	256
3x	45g	384
4x	60g	512
Weight: 26g (medium slice)		

20g CARBS   **150 CALS**

	CARBS	CALS
2x	40g	300
3x	60g	450
4x	80g	600
Weight: 36g (thick slice)		

25g CARBS   **172 CALS**

	CARBS	CALS
2x	50g	344
3x	75g	516
4x	100g	688
Weight: 46g (extra thick slice)		

Toast with Honey

8g CARBS — 58 CALS

	CARBS	CALS
2x	16g	116
3x	24g	174
4x	32g	232

Weight: 13g (medium slice)

16g CARBS — 114 CALS

	CARBS	CALS
2x	32g	228
3x	48g	342
4x	64g	456

Weight: 26g (medium slice)

21g CARBS — 136 CALS

	CARBS	CALS
2x	42g	272
3x	63g	408
4x	84g	544

Weight: 36g (thick slice)

26g CARBS — 158 CALS

	CARBS	CALS
2x	52g	316
3x	78g	474
4x	104g	632

Weight: 46g (extra thick slice)

Toast with Jam

8g CARBS   **58 CALS**

	CARBS	CALS
2x	16g	116
3x	24g	174
4x	32g	232

Weight: 13g (medium slice)

15g CARBS   **114 CALS**

	CARBS	CALS
2x	30g	228
3x	45g	342
4x	60g	456

Weight: 26g (medium slice)

20g CARBS   **136 CALS**

	CARBS	CALS
2x	40g	272
3x	60g	408
4x	80g	544

Weight: 36g (thick slice)

25g CARBS   **158 CALS**

	CARBS	CALS
2x	50g	316
3x	75g	474
4x	100g	632

Weight: 46g (extra thick slice)

Toast with Lemon Curd

8g CARBS   **58 CALS**

	CARBS	CALS
2x	16g	116
3x	24g	174
4x	32g	232

Weight: 13g (medium slice)

15g CARBS   **115 CALS**

	CARBS	CALS
2x	30g	230
3x	45g	345
4x	60g	460

Weight: 26g (medium slice)

20g CARBS   **137 CALS**

	CARBS	CALS
2x	40g	274
3x	60g	411
4x	80g	548

Weight: 36g (thick slice)

25g CARBS   **159 CALS**

	CARBS	CALS
2x	50g	318
3x	75g	477
4x	100g	636

Weight: 46g (extra thick slice)

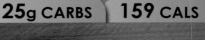

Toast with Marmalade

8g CARBS   58 CALS

	CARBS	CALS
2x	16g	116
3x	24g	174
4x	32g	232
Weight: 13g (medium slice)		

15g CARBS   114 CALS

	CARBS	CALS
2x	30g	228
3x	45g	342
4x	60g	456
Weight: 26g (medium slice)		

20g CARBS   136 CALS

	CARBS	CALS
2x	40g	272
3x	60g	408
4x	80g	544
Weight: 36g (thick slice)		

25g CARBS   158 CALS

	CARBS	CALS
2x	50g	316
3x	75g	474
4x	100g	632
Weight: 46g (extra thick slice)		

Toast with Peanut Butter

7g CARBS   67 CALS

	CARBS	CALS
2x	14g	134
3x	21g	201
4x	28g	268

Weight: 13g (medium slice)

13g CARBS   132 CALS

	CARBS	CALS
2x	26g	264
3x	39g	396
4x	52g	528

Weight: 26g (medium slice)

18g CARBS   154 CALS

	CARBS	CALS
2x	36g	308
3x	54g	462
4x	72g	616

Weight: 36g (thick slice)

23g CARBS   176 CALS

	CARBS	CALS
2x	46g	352
3x	69g	528
4x	92g	704

Weight: 46g (extra thick slice)

Bran Flakes

10g CARBS **50 CALS**

Weight: 15g

20g CARBS **99 CALS**

Weight: 30g

30g CARBS **149 CALS**

Weight: 45g

40g CARBS **198 CALS**

Weight: 60g

50g CARBS **248 CALS**

Weight: 75g

60g CARBS **300 CALS**

Weight: 91g

Chocolate Snaps

10g CARBS   **42 CALS**

Weight: 11g

20g CARBS   **81 CALS**

Weight: 21g

30g CARBS   **123 CALS**

Weight: 32g

40g CARBS   **161 CALS**

Weight: 42g

50g CARBS   **204 CALS**

Weight: 53g

60g CARBS   **246 CALS**

Weight: 64g

Corn Flakes

10g CARBS   **43 CALS**

Weight: 12g

20g CARBS   **83 CALS**

Weight: 23g

30g CARBS   **126 CALS**

Weight: 35g

40g CARBS   **169 CALS**

Weight: 47g

50g CARBS   **209 CALS**

Weight: 58g

60g CARBS   **252 CALS**

Weight: 70g

Fruit & Fibre

10g CARBS	56 CALS

Weight: 15g

20g CARBS	107 CALS

Weight: 29g

30g CARBS	163 CALS

Weight: 44g

40g CARBS	218 CALS

Weight: 59g

50g CARBS	270 CALS

Weight: 73g

60g CARBS	326 CALS

Weight: 88g

Honey Puffed Wheat

10g CARBS   **45 CALS**

Weight: 12g

20g CARBS   **87 CALS**

Weight: 23g

30g CARBS   **133 CALS**

Weight: 35g

40g CARBS   **178 CALS**

Weight: 47g

50g CARBS   **220 CALS**

Weight: 58g

60g CARBS   **265 CALS**

Weight: 70g

Malted Wheats

10g CARBS **48 CALS**

Weight: 14g

20g CARBS **95 CALS**

Weight: 28g

30g CARBS **143 CALS**

Weight: 42g

40g CARBS **190 CALS**

Weight: 56g

50g CARBS **238 CALS**

Weight: 70g

60g CARBS **286 CALS**

Weight: 84g

Muesli

20g CARBS   **110 CALS**

Weight: 30g

40g CARBS   **220 CALS**

Weight: 60g

60g CARBS   **329 CALS**

Weight: 90g

80g CARBS   **436 CALS**

Weight: 119g

100g CARBS   **545 CALS**

Weight: 149g

120g CARBS   **655 CALS**

Weight: 179g

Multigrain Hoops

10g CARBS   **48** CALS

Weight: 13g

15g CARBS   **73** CALS

Weight: 20g

20g CARBS   **99** CALS

Weight: 27g

25g CARBS   **121** CALS

Weight: 33g

30g CARBS   **147** CALS

Weight: 40g

35g CARBS   **172** CALS

Weight: 47g

Porridge (made with milk)

10g CARBS **87 CALS**

Weight: 75g

20g CARBS **168 CALS**

Weight: 145g

30g CARBS **255 CALS**

Weight: 220g

40g CARBS **336 CALS**

Weight: 290g

50g CARBS **423 CALS**

Weight: 365g

60g CARBS **505 CALS**

Weight: 435g

Raisin Bites

15g CARBS	72 CALS

Weight: 22g

30g CARBS	144 CALS

Weight: 44g

45g CARBS	213 CALS

Weight: 65g

60g CARBS	284 CALS

Weight: 87g

75g CARBS	353 CALS

Weight: 108g

90g CARBS	425 CALS

Weight: 130g

Rice Snaps

10g CARBS **42 CALS**

Weight: 11g

20g CARBS **88 CALS**

Weight: 23g

30g CARBS **130 CALS**

Weight: 34g

40g CARBS **176 CALS**

Weight: 46g

50g CARBS **218 CALS**

Weight: 57g

60g CARBS **264 CALS**

Weight: 69g

Special Flakes with Berries

10g CARBS	47 CALS

Weight: 13g

20g CARBS	95 CALS

Weight: 26g

30g CARBS	146 CALS

Weight: 40g

40g CARBS	193 CALS

Weight: 53g

50g CARBS	241 CALS

Weight: 66g

60g CARBS	292 CALS

Weight: 80g

Wheat Biscuit

13g CARBS   **64 CALS**

	CARBS	CALS
2x	26g	128
3x	39g	192
4x	52g	256
Weight: 19g		

Wheat Pillow

15g CARBS   **75 CALS**

	CARBS	CALS
2x	30g	150
3x	45g	225
4x	60g	300
Weight: 22g		

Oat Biscuit

13g CARBS   **75 CALS**

	CARBS	CALS
2x	26g	150
3x	39g	225
4x	52g	300
Weight: 20g		

Milk (semi-skimmed)

5g CARBS   **46 CALS**

	CARBS	CALS
2x	10g	92
3x	15g	138
4x	20g	184
Weight: 100g		

Eggy Bread

5g CARBS	79 CALS		10g CARBS	157 CALS

	CARBS	CALS
2x	10g	158
3x	15g	237
4x	20g	316
Weight: 25g		

	CARBS	CALS
2x	20g	314
3x	30g	471
4x	40g	628
Weight: 50g		

Fried Bread

5g CARBS	80 CALS		10g CARBS	160 CALS

	CARBS	CALS
2x	10g	160
3x	15g	240
4x	20g	320
Weight: 15g		

	CARBS	CALS
2x	20g	320
3x	30g	480
4x	40g	640
Weight: 30g		

Breakfast Tart

35g CARBS   **205 CALS**

	CARBS	CALS
2x	70g	410
3x	105g	615
4x	140g	820
Weight: 52g		

Scotch Pancake

15g CARBS   **87 CALS**

	CARBS	CALS
2x	30g	174
3x	45g	261
4x	60g	348
Weight: 31g		

Waffle (sweet)

20g CARBS   **166 CALS**

	CARBS	CALS
2x	40g	332
3x	60g	498
4x	80g	664
Weight: 38g		

30g CARBS   **258 CALS**

	CARBS	CALS
2x	60g	516
3x	90g	774
4x	120g	1032
Weight: 59g		

Pancake (plain)

5g CARBS   **60 CALS**

	CARBS	CALS
2x	10g	120
3x	15g	180
4x	20g	240
Weight: 22g		

10g CARBS   **117 CALS**

	CARBS	CALS
2x	20g	234
3x	30g	351
4x	40g	468
Weight: 43g		

15g CARBS   **169 CALS**

	CARBS	CALS
2x	30g	338
3x	45g	507
4x	60g	676
Weight: 62g		

20g CARBS   **232 CALS**

	CARBS	CALS
2x	40g	464
3x	60g	696
4x	80g	928
Weight: 85g		

Pancake with Chocolate Spread

10g CARBS   104 CALS

	CARBS	CALS
2x	20g	208
3x	30g	312
4x	40g	416
Weight: 30g		

15g CARBS   161 CALS

	CARBS	CALS
2x	30g	322
3x	45g	483
4x	60g	644
Weight: 51g		

25g CARBS   257 CALS

	CARBS	CALS
2x	50g	514
3x	75g	771
4x	100g	1028
Weight: 78g		

30g CARBS   320 CALS

	CARBS	CALS
2x	60g	640
3x	90g	960
4x	120g	1280
Weight: 101g		

Pancake with Maple Syrup

10g CARBS   81 CALS

	CARBS	CALS
2x	20g	162
3x	30g	243
4x	40g	324
Weight: 30g		

15g CARBS   138 CALS

	CARBS	CALS
2x	30g	276
3x	45g	414
4x	60g	552
Weight: 51g		

25g CARBS   211 CALS

	CARBS	CALS
2x	50g	422
3x	75g	633
4x	100g	844
Weight: 78g		

30g CARBS   274 CALS

	CARBS	CALS
2x	60g	548
3x	90g	822
4x	120g	1096
Weight: 101g		

Pancake with Sugar & Lemon

10g CARBS   80 CALS

	CARBS	CALS
2x	20g	160
3x	30g	240
4x	40g	320
Weight: 22g		

15g CARBS   137 CALS

	CARBS	CALS
2x	30g	274
3x	45g	411
4x	60g	548
Weight: 43g		

25g CARBS   209 CALS

	CARBS	CALS
2x	50g	418
3x	75g	627
4x	100g	836
Weight: 62g		

30g CARBS   272 CALS

	CARBS	CALS
2x	60g	544
3x	90g	816
4x	120g	1088
Weight: 85g		

Greek Yoghurt

5g CARBS   **90** CALS

Weight: 85g

Natural Yoghurt

5g CARBS   **55** CALS

Weight: 70g

10g CARBS   **180** CALS

Weight: 170g

15g CARBS   **150** CALS

Weight: 190g

15g CARBS   **276** CALS

Weight: 260g

25g CARBS   **253** CALS

Weight: 320g

Baklava

| 8g CARBS | 64 CALS |

	CARBS	CALS
2x	16g	128
3x	24g	192
4x	32g	256
Weight: 20g		

| 11g CARBS | 90 CALS |

	CARBS	CALS
2x	22g	180
3x	33g	270
4x	44g	360
Weight: 28g		

| 6g CARBS | 45 CALS |

	CARBS	CALS
2x	12g	90
3x	18g	135
4x	24g	180
Weight: 14g		

| 10g CARBS | 84 CALS |

	CARBS	CALS
2x	20g	168
3x	30g	252
4x	40g	336
Weight: 26g		

Bakewell Tart

15g CARBS | **155 CALS**

Weight: 34g

20g CARBS | **205 CALS**

Weight: 45g

40g CARBS | **424 CALS**

Weight: 93g

Carrot Cake

20g CARBS | **190 CALS**

Weight: 53g

40g CARBS | **384 CALS**

Weight: 107g

60g CARBS | **578 CALS**

Weight: 161g

Chocolate Cake

20g CARBS   **182** CALS

Weight: 40g

35g CARBS   **319** CALS

Weight: 70g

70g CARBS   **629** CALS

Weight: 138g

Fruit Cake

15g CARBS   **92** CALS

Weight: 26g

35g CARBS   **212** CALS

Weight: 60g

70g CARBS   **428** CALS

Weight: 121g

Ginger Cake

15g CARBS   **91 CALS**

Weight: 24g

25g CARBS   **152 CALS**

Weight: 40g

35g CARBS   **213 CALS**

Weight: 56g

Malt Loaf

20g CARBS   **93 CALS**

Weight: 30g

40g CARBS   **189 CALS**

Weight: 61g

60g CARBS   **282 CALS**

Weight: 91g

Swiss Roll

20g CARBS   **118 CALS**

Weight: 35g

40g CARBS   **233 CALS**

Weight: 69g

60g CARBS   **347 CALS**

Weight: 103g

Victoria Sponge

20g CARBS   **158 CALS**

Weight: 44g

35g CARBS   **277 CALS**

Weight: 77g

70g CARBS   **558 CALS**

Weight: 155g

Apple Danish

45g CARBS | **298 CALS**

Weight: 87g

Choc Chip Twist

40g CARBS | **357 CALS**

Weight: 85g

Cinnamon Swirl

40g CARBS | **285 CALS**

Weight: 79g

Fruit Trellis

20g CARBS | **152 CALS**

Weight: 58g

Pain au Raisin

35g CARBS | **273 CALS**

Weight: 95g

Pecan Plait

35g CARBS | **365 CALS**

Weight: 81g

Chocolate Éclair

15g CARBS   **222 CALS**

Weight: 56g

Corn Flake Cake

10g CARBS   **251 CALS**

Weight: 54g

Cup Cake

40g CARBS   **199 CALS**

Weight: 56g

Custard Slice

40g CARBS   **314 CALS**

Weight: 106g

Custard Tart

30g CARBS   **255 CALS**

Weight: 92g

Mini Battenburg

15g CARBS   **111 CALS**

Weight: 30g

Choc Ring Doughnut

25g CARBS | **201 CALS**

Weight: 49g

Glazed Ring Doughnut

25g CARBS | **176 CALS**

Weight: 46g

Jam Doughnut

35g CARBS | **239 CALS**

Weight: 71g

Mini Doughnut

5g CARBS | **44 CALS**

Weight: 11g

Sprinkle Ring Doughnut

25g CARBS | **212 CALS**

Weight: 58g

Sugar Ring Doughnut

30g CARBS | **263 CALS**

Weight: 66g

Fresh Cream Doughnut

25g CARBS **228** CALS

Weight: 69g

Yum Yum

35g CARBS **293** CALS

Weight: 70g

Blueberry Muffin

10g CARBS **100** CALS

Weight: 25g

40g CARBS **406** CALS

Weight: 102g

Chocolate Muffin

15g CARBS **108** CALS

Weight: 28g

55g CARBS **404** CALS

Weight: 105g

Flapjack

| 30g CARBS | 242 CALS | 50g CARBS | 397 CALS |

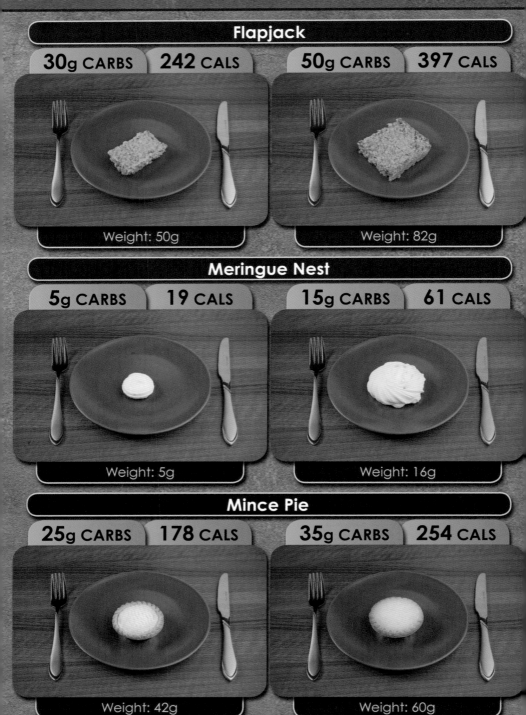

Weight: 50g

Weight: 82g

Meringue Nest

| 5g CARBS | 19 CALS | 15g CARBS | 61 CALS |

Weight: 5g

Weight: 16g

Mince Pie

| 25g CARBS | 178 CALS | 35g CARBS | 254 CALS |

Weight: 42g

Weight: 60g

Belgian Bun

65g CARBS　　**419** CALS

Weight: 116g

Cheese Scone

25g CARBS　　**238** CALS

Weight: 68g

Fruit Scone

20g CARBS　　**120** CALS

Weight: 38g

35g CARBS　　**209** CALS

Weight: 66g

Hot Cross Bun

30g CARBS　　**158** CALS

Weight: 51g

Iced Bun

20g CARBS　　**124** CALS

Weight: 37g

Apple Pie

20g CARBS   **141 CALS**

Weight: 50g

40g CARBS   **282 CALS**

Weight: 100g

60g CARBS   **426 CALS**

Weight: 151g

80g CARBS   **567 CALS**

Weight: 201g

100g CARBS   **711 CALS**

Weight: 252g

120g CARBS   **852 CALS**

Weight: 302g

Apple & Rhubarb Crumble

20g CARBS   **119 CALS**

Weight: 60g

40g CARBS   **232 CALS**

Weight: 117g

60g CARBS   **347 CALS**

Weight: 175g

80g CARBS   **465 CALS**

Weight: 235g

100g CARBS   **584 CALS**

Weight: 295g

120g CARBS   **697 CALS**

Weight: 352g

Apple Strudel

15g CARBS   **126 CALS**

Weight: 45g

30g CARBS   **252 CALS**

Weight: 90g

45g CARBS   **378 CALS**

Weight: 135g

60g CARBS   **510 CALS**

Weight: 182g

75g CARBS   **638 CALS**

Weight: 228g

90g CARBS   **762 CALS**

Weight: 272g

Banoffee Pie

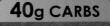

20g CARBS **146 CALS**

Weight: 43g

40g CARBS **303 CALS**

Weight: 89g

60g CARBS **452 CALS**

Weight: 133g

80g CARBS **598 CALS**

Weight: 176g

100g CARBS **748 CALS**

Weight: 220g

120g CARBS **901 CALS**

Weight: 265g

Black Forest Gateau

10g CARBS   **90 CALS**

Weight: 35g

20g CARBS   **175 CALS**

Weight: 68g

30g CARBS   **257 CALS**

Weight: 100g

40g CARBS   **347 CALS**

Weight: 135g

50g CARBS   **432 CALS**

Weight: 168g

60g CARBS   **514 CALS**

Weight: 200g

Bread & Butter Pudding

10g CARBS   **98 CALS**

Weight: 40g

20g CARBS   **199 CALS**

Weight: 81g

30g CARBS   **300 CALS**

Weight: 122g

40g CARBS   **403 CALS**

Weight: 164g

50g CARBS   **504 CALS**

Weight: 205g

60g CARBS   **605 CALS**

Weight: 246g

Brownie

25g CARBS   **200** CALS

Weight: 45g

45g CARBS   **364** CALS

Weight: 82g

70g CARBS   **564** CALS

Weight: 127g

90g CARBS   **728** CALS

Weight: 164g

115g CARBS   **928** CALS

Weight: 209g

135g CARBS   **1092** CALS

Weight: 246g

Cheesecake

15g CARBS   **155 CALS**

Weight: 50g

30g CARBS   **310 CALS**

Weight: 100g

45g CARBS   **465 CALS**

Weight: 150g

60g CARBS   **620 CALS**

Weight: 200g

75g CARBS   **775 CALS**

Weight: 250g

90g CARBS   **930 CALS**

Weight: 300g

Chocolate Torte

10g CARBS   **107 CALS**

Weight: 33g

20g CARBS   **215 CALS**

Weight: 66g

30g CARBS   **325 CALS**

Weight: 100g

40g CARBS   **432 CALS**

Weight: 133g

50g CARBS   **540 CALS**

Weight: 166g

60g CARBS   **650 CALS**

Weight: 200g

Christmas Pudding

20g CARBS   **115 CALS**

Weight: 35g

40g CARBS   **234 CALS**

Weight: 71g

60g CARBS   **349 CALS**

Weight: 106g (individual)

80g CARBS   **467 CALS**

Weight: 142g

100g CARBS   **582 CALS**

Weight: 177g

120g CARBS   **704 CALS**

Weight: 214g

Custard (made with whole milk)

10g CARBS	70 CALS	20g CARBS	140 CALS

Weight: 60g   Weight: 120g

30g CARBS	211 CALS	40g CARBS	281 CALS

Weight: 180g   Weight: 240g

50g CARBS	351 CALS	60g CARBS	421 CALS

Weight: 300g   Weight: 360g

Ice Cream (vanilla)

10g CARBS · **78 CALS**

Weight: 40g

Lemon Sorbet

15g CARBS · **59 CALS**

Weight: 45g

20g CARBS · **155 CALS**

Weight: 80g

30g CARBS · **115 CALS**

Weight: 88g

30g CARBS · **235 CALS**

Weight: 121g

45g CARBS · **173 CALS**

Weight: 132g

Choc Ice

| 15g CARBS | 144 CALS |

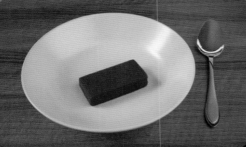

Weight: 52g

Crème Brûlée

| 15g CARBS | 343 CALS |

Weight: 104g

Chocolate & Nut Cone

| 25g CARBS | 190 CALS |

Weight: 73g

Panna Cotta

| 25g CARBS | 413 CALS |

Weight: 145g

Ice Cream Lolly

| 25g CARBS | 308 CALS |

Weight: 89g

Strawberry Tartlet

| 35g CARBS | 330 CALS |

Weight: 132g

Jelly

10g CARBS   **40 CALS**

Weight: 65g

20g CARBS   **79 CALS**

Weight: 130g

30g CARBS   **122 CALS**

Weight: 200g

40g CARBS   **162 CALS**

Weight: 265g

50g CARBS   **201 CALS**

Weight: 330g

60g CARBS   **244 CALS**

Weight: 400g

Lemon Meringue Pie

20g CARBS   **140 CALS**

Weight: 44g

40g CARBS   **281 CALS**

Weight: 88g

60g CARBS   **415 CALS**

Weight: 130g

80g CARBS   **558 CALS**

Weight: 175g

100g CARBS   **695 CALS**

Weight: 218g

120g CARBS   **836 CALS**

Weight: 262g

Mousse (chocolate)

10g CARBS	70 CALS

Weight: 50g

20g CARBS	139 CALS

Weight: 100g

30g CARBS	209 CALS

Weight: 150g

40g CARBS	278 CALS

Weight: 200g

50g CARBS	348 CALS

Weight: 250g

60g CARBS	417 CALS

Weight: 300g

Profiteroles

10g CARBS   **138** CALS

Weight: 40g

20g CARBS   **277** CALS

Weight: 80g

30g CARBS   **415** CALS

Weight: 120g

40g CARBS   **557** CALS

Weight: 161g

50g CARBS   **709** CALS

Weight: 205g

60g CARBS   **848** CALS

Weight: 245g

Rice Pudding

10g CARBS — **62 CALS**

Weight: 70g

20g CARBS — **125 CALS**

Weight: 140g

30g CARBS — **191 CALS**

Weight: 215g

40g CARBS — **254 CALS**

Weight: 285g

50g CARBS — **316 CALS**

Weight: 355g

60g CARBS — **378 CALS**

Weight: 425g

Roulade

20g CARBS   **133 CALS**

Weight: 38g

40g CARBS   **266 CALS**

Weight: 76g

60g CARBS   **399 CALS**

Weight: 114g

80g CARBS   **539 CALS**

Weight: 154g

100g CARBS   **672 CALS**

Weight: 192g

120g CARBS   **805 CALS**

Weight: 230g

Spotted Dick

25g CARBS   **180 CALS**

Weight: 52g

50g CARBS   **363 CALS**

Weight: 105g (individual)

75g CARBS   **547 CALS**

Weight: 158g

100g CARBS   **730 CALS**

Weight: 211g

125g CARBS   **913 CALS**

Weight: 264g

150g CARBS   **1097 CALS**

Weight: 317g

Sticky Toffee Pudding

15g CARBS   **112 CALS**

Weight: 31g

30g CARBS   **223 CALS**

Weight: 62g

45g CARBS   **338 CALS**

Weight: 94g

60g CARBS   **450 CALS**

Weight: 125g

75g CARBS   **569 CALS**

Weight: 158g

90g CARBS   **680 CALS**

Weight: 189g

Strawberry Delight

5g CARBS   **38 CALS**

Weight: 33g

15g CARBS   **116 CALS**

Weight: 100g

25g CARBS   **193 CALS**

Weight: 166g

35g CARBS   **270 CALS**

Weight: 233g

45g CARBS   **348 CALS**

Weight: 300g

55g CARBS   **427 CALS**

Weight: 368g

Summer Pudding

10g CARBS   **43** CALS

Weight: 45g

20g CARBS   **89** CALS

Weight: 94g

30g CARBS   **133** CALS

Weight: 140g (individual)

40g CARBS   **176** CALS

Weight: 185g

50g CARBS   **221** CALS

Weight: 233g

60g CARBS   **266** CALS

Weight: 280g

Tiramisu

15g CARBS **110 CALS**

Weight: 45g

30g CARBS **221 CALS**

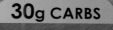

Weight: 90g

45g CARBS **328 CALS**

Weight: 134g

60g CARBS **436 CALS**

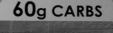

Weight: 178g

75g CARBS **544 CALS**

Weight: 222g

90g CARBS **649 CALS**

Weight: 265g

Trifle

15g CARBS   **193 CALS**

Weight: 55g

30g CARBS   **378 CALS**

Weight: 108g

45g CARBS   **567 CALS**

Weight: 162g

60g CARBS   **753 CALS**

Weight: 215g

75g CARBS   **945 CALS**

Weight: 270g

90g CARBS   **1138 CALS**

Weight: 325g

Apple Juice

| 16g CARBS | 28g CARBS | 57g CARBS |
| 61 CALS | 109 CALS | 218 CALS |

| 160ml | 287ml (half pint) | 574ml (pint) |

Cranberry Juice

| 23g CARBS | 41g CARBS | 83g CARBS |
| 98 CALS | 175 CALS | 350 CALS |

| 160ml | 287ml (half pint) | 574ml (pint) |

Grapefruit Juice

| 13g CARBS | 24g CARBS | 48g CARBS |
| 53 CALS | 95 CALS | 189 CALS |

| 160ml | 287ml (half pint) | 574ml (pint) |

Orange Juice

| 14g CARBS | 25g CARBS | 51g CARBS |
| 58 CALS | 103 CALS | 207 CALS |

  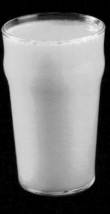

| 160ml | 287ml (half pint) | 574ml (pint) |

Pineapple Juice

17g CARBS	30g CARBS	60g CARBS
66 CALS	118 CALS	235 CALS

  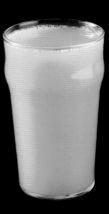

160ml	287ml (half pint)	574ml (pint)

Tomato Juice

5g CARBS	9g CARBS	17g CARBS
22 CALS	40 CALS	80 CALS

160ml	287ml (half pint)	574ml (pint)

Cola

17g CARBS	30g CARBS	60g CARBS
62 CALS	112 CALS	224 CALS

160ml	287ml (half pint)	574ml (pint)

Lucozade Energy

10g CARBS	20g CARBS	30g CARBS
39 CALS	80 CALS	119 CALS

56ml	114ml	170ml

Milk (skimmed)

7g CARBS	13g CARBS	25g CARBS
51 CALS	92 CALS	184 CALS

160ml	287ml (half pint)	574ml (pint)

Milk (semi-skimmed)

8g CARBS	14g CARBS	29g CARBS
74 CALS	132 CALS	264 CALS

160ml	287ml (half pint)	574ml (pint)

Milk (whole)

7g CARBS	13g CARBS	26g CARBS
106 CALS	189 CALS	379 CALS

160ml	287ml (half pint)	574ml (pint)

Soya Milk (sweetened)

4g CARBS	7g CARBS	14g CARBS
69 CALS	123 CALS	247 CALS

160ml	287ml (half pint)	574ml (pint)

Fruit Smoothie

18g CARBS	83 CALS

160ml

63g CARBS	298 CALS

574ml (pint)

Milkshake (made with powder & semi-skimmed milk)

32g CARBS	198 CALS

287ml (half pint)

65g CARBS	396 CALS

574ml (pint)

Hot Chocolate

28g CARBS	185 CALS

260ml

Hot Malt Drink

34g CARBS	211 CALS

260ml

Lager

4g CARBS · **83 CALS**
287ml (half pint)

9g CARBS · **166 CALS**
574ml (pint)

Ale

9g CARBS · **80 CALS**
287ml (half pint)

17g CARBS · **161 CALS**
574ml (pint)

Stout

12g CARBS · **106 CALS**
287ml (half pint)

24g CARBS · **212 CALS**
574ml (pint)

Cider (dry)

7g CARBS | **103** CALS

287ml (half pint)

15g CARBS | **207** CALS

574ml (pint)

Cider (sweet)

12g CARBS | **121** CALS

287ml (half pint)

25g CARBS | **241** CALS

574ml (pint)

Cider (vintage)

21g CARBS | **290** CALS

287ml (half pint)

42g CARBS | **580** CALS

574ml (pint)

Sweet White Wine

7g CARBS | **118 CALS**

125ml (small glass)

15g CARBS | **235 CALS**

250ml (large glass)

Advocaat

14g CARBS | **136 CALS**

50ml

Vermouth (sweet)

8g CARBS | **76 CALS**

50ml

Port

6g CARBS | **79 CALS**

50ml

Sweet Liqueur

8g CARBS | **64 CALS**

25ml

WKD

| **35g CARBS** | **207 CALS** |

	CARBS	CALS
2x	70g	414
3x	105g	621
4x	140g	828
275ml bottle		

WKD Core (cider)

| **47g CARBS** | **325 CALS** |

	CARBS	CALS
2x	94g	650
3x	141g	975
4x	188g	1300
500ml bottle		

Energy Drink

14g CARBS	**28g CARBS**
56 CALS	**113 CALS**

| 125ml (half can) | 250ml (full can) |

Apricot (fresh)

4g CARBS	17 CALS

Weight: 55g

8g CARBS	34 CALS

Weight: 110g

12g CARBS	51 CALS

Weight: 165g

Apricot (dried)

10g CARBS	44 CALS

Weight: 28g

20g CARBS	87 CALS

Weight: 55g

30g CARBS	130 CALS

Weight: 82g

Apple

10g CARBS   **40 CALS**

Weight: 85g

Blueberries

5g CARBS   **21 CALS**

Weight: 40g

15g CARBS   **62 CALS**

Weight: 131g

15g CARBS   **68 CALS**

Weight: 130g

20g CARBS   **80 CALS**

Weight: 170g

25g CARBS   **112 CALS**

Weight: 215g

Banana

15g CARBS	**60** CALS

Weight: 63g (without skin)

15g CARBS	**60** CALS

Weight: 97g (with skin)

20g CARBS	**81** CALS

Weight: 85g (without skin)

20g CARBS	**81** CALS

Weight: 130g (with skin)

30g CARBS	**122** CALS

Weight: 128g (without skin)

30g CARBS	**122** CALS

Weight: 190g (with skin)

Cherries

5g CARBS   **20** CALS

Weight: 50g (with stones)

Clementine

5g CARBS   **22** CALS

Weight: 80g

10g CARBS   **39** CALS

Weight: 100g (with stones)

10g CARBS   **45** CALS

Weight: 160g

15g CARBS   **62** CALS

Weight: 160g (with stones)

Satsuma

5g CARBS   **22** CALS

Weight: 85g

Fruit Cocktail (in juice)

5g CARBS	22 CALS

Weight: 75g

15g CARBS	61 CALS

Weight: 210g (half tin)

30g CARBS	122 CALS

Weight: 420g (full tin)

Grapefruit

5g CARBS	24 CALS

Weight: 119g (half)

10g CARBS	46 CALS

Weight: 228g (whole)

10g CARBS	46 CALS

Weight: 140g (whole)

Grapes (seedless)

10g CARBS   **39 CALS**

Weight: 65g

20g CARBS   **78 CALS**

Weight: 130g

30g CARBS   **117 CALS**

Weight: 195g

40g CARBS   **156 CALS**

Weight: 260g

50g CARBS   **195 CALS**

Weight: 325g

60g CARBS   **234 CALS**

Weight: 390g

Kiwi

5g CARBS | **24** CALS

Weight: 55g (1 kiwi with skin)

5g CARBS | **24** CALS

Weight: 51g (1 kiwi)

10g CARBS | **47** CALS

Weight: 95g (2 kiwis)

Mango

10g CARBS | **40** CALS

Weight: 70g

20g CARBS | **80** CALS

Weight: 140g

30g CARBS | **120** CALS

Weight: 210g

Melon (honeydew)

10g CARBS | **42** CALS

Weight: 150g

20g CARBS | **84** CALS

Weight: 300g

30g CARBS | **126** CALS

Weight: 450g

Watermelon

10g CARBS | **43** CALS

Weight: 140g

20g CARBS | **87** CALS

Weight: 280g

30g CARBS | **130** CALS

Weight: 420g

Orange

| 4g CARBS | 18 CALS |

Weight: 71g

| 7g CARBS | 30 CALS |

Weight: 115g

| 10g CARBS | 45 CALS |

Weight: 172g

Papaya

| 5g CARBS | 24 CALS |

Weight: 90g

| 10g CARBS | 49 CALS |

Weight: 180g

| 15g CARBS | 73 CALS |

Weight: 270g

Peach (fresh)

5g CARBS	23 CALS

Weight: 70g (without stone)

10g CARBS	46 CALS

Weight: 138g

15g CARBS	66 CALS

Weight: 200g

Peach (tinned in juice)

10g CARBS	39 CALS

Weight: 100g

20g CARBS	80 CALS

Weight: 205g (half tin)

40g CARBS	160 CALS

Weight: 410g (full tin)

Pear

10g CARBS   **42 CALS**

Weight: 104g

20g CARBS   **78 CALS**

Weight: 195g

30g CARBS   **118 CALS**

Weight: 295g

Pear (tinned in juice)

10g CARBS   **38 CALS**

Weight: 115g

20g CARBS   **76 CALS**

Weight: 230g

30g CARBS   **117 CALS**

Weight: 355g (full tin)

Pineapple (fresh)

4g CARBS   **16 CALS**

Weight: 40g

8g CARBS   **33 CALS**

Weight: 80g

12g CARBS   **49 CALS**

Weight: 120g

16g CARBS   **66 CALS**

Weight: 160g

20g CARBS   **82 CALS**

Weight: 200g

24g CARBS   **98 CALS**

Weight: 240g

Pineapple (tinned in juice)

5g CARBS	19 CALS

Weight: 40g

10g CARBS	38 CALS

Weight: 80g

20g CARBS	75 CALS

Weight: 160g

30g CARBS	115 CALS

Weight: 245g

40g CARBS	155 CALS

Weight: 330g

50g CARBS	193 CALS

Weight: 410g (full tin)

Pomegranate

5g CARBS **20** CALS

Weight: 40g

10g CARBS **43** CALS

Weight: 85g

15g CARBS **64** CALS

Weight: 125g

Prune

10g CARBS **42** CALS

Weight: 30g

20g CARBS **85** CALS

Weight: 60g

30g CARBS **125** CALS

Weight: 89g

Plum

5g CARBS	20 CALS

10g CARBS	40 CALS

CARBS	CALS
10g	40
15g	60
20g	80
Weight: 55g	

	CARBS	CALS
2x	20g	80
3x	30g	120
4x	40g	160
	Weight: 110g	

Nectarine

7g CARBS	32 CALS

15g CARBS	66 CALS

CARBS	CALS
14g	64
21g	96
28g	128
Weight: 80g (without stone)	

	CARBS	CALS
2x	30g	132
3x	45g	198
4x	60g	264
	Weight: 165g	

Raspberries

5g CARBS | **26** CALS

Weight: 105g

Strawberries

5g CARBS | **23** CALS

Weight: 85g

10g CARBS | **53** CALS

Weight: 210g

15g CARBS | **68** CALS

Weight: 250g

15g CARBS | **80** CALS

Weight: 320g

25g CARBS | **111** CALS

Weight: 410g

Raisins

10g CARBS **41** CALS

Weight: 15g

20g CARBS **79** CALS

Weight: 29g

30g CARBS **120** CALS

Weight: 44g

Sultanas

10g CARBS **41** CALS

Weight: 15g

20g CARBS **80** CALS

Weight: 29g

30g CARBS **118** CALS

Weight: 43g

Beans on Toast

20g CARBS   **148 CALS**

Weight: 92g

30g CARBS   **202 CALS**

Weight: 157g

40g CARBS   **257 CALS**

Weight: 222g

50g CARBS   **350 CALS**

Weight: 249g (half tin of beans)

65g CARBS   **432 CALS**

Weight: 379g

80g CARBS   **514 CALS**

Weight: 444g (full tin of beans)

Chicken Goujons, Potato Faces & Peas

20g CARBS | **179** CALS

Weight: 100g

35g CARBS | **319** CALS

Weight: 178g

55g CARBS | **499** CALS

Weight: 278g

70g CARBS | **639** CALS

Weight: 356g

90g CARBS | **818** CALS

Weight: 456g

105g CARBS | **958** CALS

Weight: 534g

Chilli con Carne with White Rice

15g CARBS	122 CALS

Weight: 122g

40g CARBS	280 CALS

Weight: 266g

65g CARBS	443 CALS

Weight: 413g

90g CARBS	607 CALS

Weight: 565g

115g CARBS	774 CALS

Weight: 720g

140g CARBS	934 CALS

Weight: 865g

Corned Beef Hash

10g CARBS | **100 CALS**

Weight: 100g

20g CARBS | **200 CALS**

Weight: 200g

30g CARBS | **300 CALS**

Weight: 300g

40g CARBS | **400 CALS**

Weight: 400g

50g CARBS | **500 CALS**

Weight: 500g

60g CARBS | **600 CALS**

Weight: 600g

Curry (chicken) with White Rice

10g CARBS   **145 CALS**

Weight: 136g

35g CARBS   **387 CALS**

Weight: 358g

55g CARBS   **576 CALS**

Weight: 526g

80g CARBS   **805 CALS**

Weight: 733g

100g CARBS   **1006 CALS**

Weight: 915g

125g CARBS   **1259 CALS**

Weight: 1147g

Curry (lentil) with Brown Rice

20g CARBS	178 CALS

Weight: 125g

50g CARBS	399 CALS

Weight: 280g

80g CARBS	621 CALS

Weight: 437g

110g CARBS	852 CALS

Weight: 599g

140g CARBS	1075 CALS

Weight: 756g

170g CARBS	1300 CALS

Weight: 914g

Curry (veg & potato) with White Rice

20g CARBS   **122 CALS**

Weight: 122g

50g CARBS   **286 CALS**

Weight: 272g

80g CARBS   **451 CALS**

Weight: 423g

110g CARBS   **618 CALS**

Weight: 577g

140g CARBS   **785 CALS**

Weight: 731g

170g CARBS   **951 CALS**

Weight: 885g

Fish Fingers, Oven Chips & Beans

30g CARBS   **236** CALS

Weight: 131g

50g CARBS   **393** CALS

Weight: 229g

70g CARBS   **544** CALS

Weight: 325g

90g CARBS   **705** CALS

Weight: 425g

110g CARBS   **866** CALS

Weight: 528g

130g CARBS   **1021** CALS

Weight: 625g

Fish Pie

10g CARBS   **144 CALS**

Weight: 125g

20g CARBS   **288 CALS**

Weight: 250g

30g CARBS   **437 CALS**

Weight: 380g

40g CARBS   **581 CALS**

Weight: 505g

50g CARBS   **725 CALS**

Weight: 630g

60g CARBS   **874 CALS**

Weight: 760g

Lasagne

10g CARBS **135 CALS**

Weight: 80g

25g CARBS **330 CALS**

Weight: 195g

40g CARBS **532 CALS**

Weight: 315g

55g CARBS **727 CALS**

Weight: 430g

70g CARBS **921 CALS**

Weight: 545g

85g CARBS **1124 CALS**

Weight: 665g

Macaroni Cheese

15g CARBS   **166 CALS**

Weight: 80g

30g CARBS   **337 CALS**

Weight: 163g

40g CARBS   **460 CALS**

Weight: 222g

55g CARBS   **629 CALS**

Weight: 304g

70g CARBS   **797 CALS**

Weight: 385g

85g CARBS   **963 CALS**

Weight: 465g

Enchilada

32g CARBS   **318 CALS**

	CARBS	CALS
2x	64g	636
3x	96g	954
4x	128g	1272
Weight: 146g		

Fajita

30g CARBS   **238 CALS**

	CARBS	CALS
2x	60g	476
3x	90g	714
4x	120g	952
Weight: 160g		

Quesadilla

18g CARBS   **159 CALS**

	CARBS	CALS
2x	36g	318
3x	54g	477
4x	72g	636
Weight: 74g		

Taco

11g CARBS   **219 CALS**

	CARBS	CALS
2x	22g	438
3x	33g	657
4x	44g	876
Weight: 80g		

Pasta Bake

15g CARBS | **108 CALS**

Weight: 70g

30g CARBS | **220 CALS**

Weight: 143g

45g CARBS | **330 CALS**

Weight: 214g

60g CARBS | **439 CALS**

Weight: 285g

75g CARBS | **547 CALS**

Weight: 355g

90g CARBS | **656 CALS**

Weight: 426g

Pasta Meal

10g CARBS **115 CALS**

Weight: 65g

25g CARBS **294 CALS**

Weight: 166g

40g CARBS **473 CALS**

Weight: 267g

50g CARBS **604 CALS**

Weight: 341g

65g CARBS **782 CALS**

Weight: 442g

80g CARBS **961 CALS**

Weight: 543g

Chicken & Bacon Pie

50g CARBS   **700 CALS**

Weight: 264g

Steak Pie

40g CARBS   **564 CALS**

Weight: 244g

Steak & Kidney Pudding

40g CARBS   **437 CALS**

Weight: 182g

Top Crust Pie

25g CARBS   **362 CALS**

Weight: 264g

Steak & Potato Pie

25g CARBS   **307 CALS**

Weight: 130g

50g CARBS   **625 CALS**

Weight: 265g

Pizza (deep pan - oven baked)

20g CARBS　159 CALS

	CARBS	CALS
2x	40g	318
3x	60g	477
4x	80g	636
Weight: 65g		

40g CARBS　319 CALS

	CARBS	CALS
2x	80g	638
3x	120g	957
4x	160g	1276
Weight: 130g		

60g CARBS　478 CALS

	CARBS	CALS
2x	120g	956
3x	180g	1434
4x	240g	1912
Weight: 195g		

80g CARBS　632 CALS

	CARBS	CALS
2x	160g	1264
3x	240g	1896
4x	320g	2528
Weight: 258g		

Pizza (thin crust - oven baked)

10g CARBS   104 CALS

	CARBS	CALS
2x	20g	208
3x	30g	312
4x	40g	416
Weight: 40g		

20g CARBS   196 CALS

	CARBS	CALS
2x	40g	392
3x	60g	588
4x	80g	784
Weight: 75g		

30g CARBS   300 CALS

	CARBS	CALS
2x	60g	600
3x	90g	900
4x	120g	1200
Weight: 115g		

40g CARBS   405 CALS

	CARBS	CALS
2x	80g	810
3x	120g	1215
4x	160g	1620
Weight: 155g		

Quiche Lorraine, Salad & Coleslaw

15g CARBS   **279 CALS**

Weight: 145g

25g CARBS   **465 CALS**

Weight: 215g

40g CARBS   **741 CALS**

Weight: 340g

50g CARBS   **914 CALS**

Weight: 405g

65g CARBS   **1190 CALS**

Weight: 535g

75g CARBS   **1376 CALS**

Weight: 605g

Risotto

20g CARBS **168 CALS**

Weight: 120g

40g CARBS **337 CALS**

Weight: 241g

60g CARBS **508 CALS**

Weight: 363g

80g CARBS **679 CALS**

Weight: 485g

100g CARBS **850 CALS**

Weight: 607g

120g CARBS **1021 CALS**

Weight: 729g

Sausage, Mash & Onion Gravy

25g CARBS   **256 CALS**

Weight: 200g

50g CARBS   **508 CALS**

Weight: 395g

80g CARBS   **765 CALS**

Weight: 595g

105g CARBS   **1016 CALS**

Weight: 790g

130g CARBS   **1273 CALS**

Weight: 990g

155g CARBS   **1525 CALS**

Weight: 1185g

Shepherd's Pie

10g CARBS   **142 CALS**

Weight: 120g

20g CARBS   **283 CALS**

Weight: 240g

30g CARBS   **425 CALS**

Weight: 360g

40g CARBS   **572 CALS**

Weight: 485g

50g CARBS   **714 CALS**

Weight: 605g

60g CARBS   **861 CALS**

Weight: 730g

Chicken Noodle Soup

5g CARBS   **26 CALS**

Weight: 130g

10g CARBS   **52 CALS**

Weight: 260g

15g CARBS   **80 CALS**

Weight: 400g

Chunky Veg Soup

10g CARBS   **57 CALS**

Weight: 133g

20g CARBS   **114 CALS**

Weight: 266g

30g CARBS   **172 CALS**

Weight: 400g (full tin)

Mushroom Soup

5g CARBS   **69** CALS

Weight: 130g

Tomato Soup

10g CARBS   **82** CALS

Weight: 135g

10g CARBS   **138** CALS

Weight: 260g

20g CARBS   **168** CALS

Weight: 275g

15g CARBS   **207** CALS

Weight: 390g (full tin)

30g CARBS   **250** CALS

Weight: 410g (full tin)

Spaghetti Bolognaise

15g CARBS **129 CALS**

Weight: 153g

40g CARBS **303 CALS**

Weight: 335g

65g CARBS **478 CALS**

Weight: 518g

90g CARBS **657 CALS**

Weight: 703g

115g CARBS **836 CALS**

Weight: 891g

140g CARBS **1018 CALS**

Weight: 1084g

Stew & Dumplings

20g CARBS **204 CALS**

Weight: 140g

40g CARBS **397 CALS**

Weight: 265g

65g CARBS **658 CALS**

Weight: 490g

85g CARBS **855 CALS**

Weight: 620g

105g CARBS **1062 CALS**

Weight: 765g

125g CARBS **1259 CALS**

Weight: 895g

Stir-fry (chicken)

10g CARBS	80 CALS

Weight: 70g

20g CARBS	160 CALS

Weight: 140g

30g CARBS	234 CALS

Weight: 205g

40g CARBS	314 CALS

Weight: 275g

50g CARBS	393 CALS

Weight: 345g

60g CARBS	469 CALS

Weight: 411g

Sushi

8g CARBS   **56 CALS**

	CARBS	CALS
2x	16g	112
3x	24g	168
4x	32g	224
Weight: 34g		

14g CARBS   **114 CALS**

	CARBS	CALS
2x	28g	228
3x	42g	342
4x	56g	456
Weight: 36g		

7g CARBS   **62 CALS**

	CARBS	CALS
2x	14g	124
3x	21g	186
4x	28g	248
Weight: 28g		

5g CARBS   **64 CALS**

	CARBS	CALS
2x	10g	128
3x	15g	192
4x	20g	256
Weight: 24g		

Toad in the Hole

20g CARBS	269 CALS

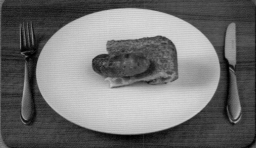

Weight: 92g

40g CARBS	534 CALS

Weight: 183g

60g CARBS	803 CALS

Weight: 275g

80g CARBS	1069 CALS

Weight: 366g

100g CARBS	1335 CALS

Weight: 457g

120g CARBS	1603 CALS

Weight: 549g

Coleslaw

5g CARBS	103 CALS

Weight: 65g

10g CARBS	207 CALS

Weight: 130g

Onion Rings

10g CARBS	78 CALS

Weight: 26g

20g CARBS	156 CALS

Weight: 52g

Potato Salad (with mayonnaise)

10g CARBS	198 CALS

Weight: 83g

20g CARBS	397 CALS

Weight: 166g

Stuffing

20g CARBS **99** CALS

Weight: 65g

40g CARBS **198** CALS

Weight: 130g

60g CARBS **296** CALS

Weight: 195g

Yorkshire Pudding

10g CARBS **83** CALS

Weight: 40g

20g CARBS **166** CALS

Weight: 80g

30g CARBS **250** CALS

Weight: 120g

Apple Chutney

10g CARBS   **38** CALS

Weight: 20g

Brown Sauce

5g CARBS   **21** CALS

Weight: 21g

Cranberry Sauce

5g CARBS   **22** CALS

Weight: 14g

Horseradish

5g CARBS   **40** CALS

Weight: 26g

Ketchup

5g CARBS   **22** CALS

Weight: 19g

Mint Sauce

5g CARBS   **21** CALS

Weight: 21g

Piccalilli

5g CARBS | **24 CALS**

Weight: 22g

Pickle

10g CARBS | **39 CALS**

Weight: 28g

Salad Cream

5g CARBS | **94 CALS**

Weight: 27g

Sweet Chilli Sauce

5g CARBS | **20 CALS**

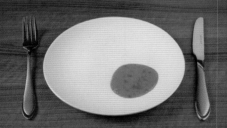

Weight: 10g

Tartar Sauce

5g CARBS | **78 CALS**

Weight: 26g

Thousand Island

5g CARBS | **116 CALS**

Weight: 36g

Fish (battered)

10g CARBS   **109 CALS**

Weight: 65g

20g CARBS   **218 CALS**

Weight: 130g

40g CARBS   **445 CALS**

Weight: 265g

Fish (breaded)

10g CARBS   **109 CALS**

Weight: 53g

20g CARBS   **218 CALS**

Weight: 106g

30g CARBS   **321 CALS**

Weight: 156g

Fish Cake

| **8g CARBS** | **98 CALS** | | **14g CARBS** | **169 CALS** |

	CARBS	CALS
2x	16g	196
3x	24g	294
4x	32g	392
Weight: 52g		

	CARBS	CALS
2x	28g	338
3x	42g	507
4x	56g	676
Weight: 90g		

Fish Finger

3g CARBS   **40 CALS**

	CARBS	CALS
2x	6g	80
3x	9g	120
4x	12g	160
Weight: 20g		

Fish Goujon

5g CARBS   **64 CALS**

	CARBS	CALS
2x	10g	128
3x	15g	192
4x	20g	256
Weight: 30g		

Scampi

20g CARBS | **221 CALS**

Weight: 70g

40g CARBS | **442 CALS**

Weight: 140g

60g CARBS | **657 CALS**

Weight: 208g

Haggis

20g CARBS | **326 CALS**

Weight: 105g

40g CARBS | **651 CALS**

Weight: 210g

60g CARBS | **977 CALS**

Weight: 315g

Black Pudding

10g CARBS   **74** CALS

	CARBS	CALS
2x	20g	148
3x	30g	222
4x	40g	296
Weight: 58g		

Chicken Goujon

5g CARBS   **77** CALS

	CARBS	CALS
2x	10g	154
3x	15g	231
4x	20g	308
Weight: 30g		

Sausage (thin)

2g CARBS   **59** CALS

	CARBS	CALS
2x	4g	118
3x	6g	177
4x	8g	236
Weight: 20g		

Sausage (thick)

5g CARBS   **162** CALS

	CARBS	CALS
2x	10g	324
3x	15g	486
4x	20g	648
Weight: 55g		

Chicken Kiev

15g CARBS | **358 CALS**

Weight: 130g

30g CARBS | **715 CALS**

Weight: 260g

Pork Pie

30g CARBS | **447 CALS**

Weight: 119g

80g CARBS | **1203 CALS**

Weight: 320g

Scotch Egg

8g CARBS | **151 CALS**

Weight: 60g

16g CARBS | **301 CALS**

Weight: 120g

Cornish Pasty

10g CARBS   **103 CALS**

Weight: 31g

50g CARBS   **538 CALS**

Weight: 162g

60g CARBS   **644 CALS**

Weight: 194g

135g CARBS   **1441 CALS**

Weight: 434g

Sausage Roll

20g CARBS   **301 CALS**

Weight: 63g

40g CARBS   **591 CALS**

Weight: 124g

Sausages & Beans (tinned)

9g CARBS   **84 CALS**

Weight: 70g

18g CARBS   **168 CALS**

Weight: 140g

27g CARBS   **252 CALS**

Weight: 210g (half tin)

37g CARBS   **342 CALS**

Weight: 285g

46g CARBS   **426 CALS**

Weight: 355g

55g CARBS   **510 CALS**

Weight: 425g (full tin)

Cassava Chips

30g CARBS   **159** CALS

Weight: 45g

60g CARBS   **321** CALS

Weight: 91g

90g CARBS   **480** CALS

Weight: 136g

120g CARBS   **642** CALS

Weight: 182g

150g CARBS   **805** CALS

Weight: 228g

180g CARBS   **960** CALS

Weight: 272g

Chips (deep fried)

10g CARBS — **79 CALS**

Weight: 33g

30g CARBS — **237 CALS**

Weight: 99g

50g CARBS — **394 CALS**

Weight: 165g

70g CARBS — **550 CALS**

Weight: 230g

90g CARBS — **705 CALS**

Weight: 295g

110g CARBS — **860 CALS**

Weight: 360g

Chips (oven)

10g CARBS	**53 CALS**

Weight: 33g

30g CARBS	**162 CALS**

Weight: 100g

50g CARBS	**272 CALS**

Weight: 168g

70g CARBS	**381 CALS**

Weight: 235g

90g CARBS	**491 CALS**

Weight: 303g

110g CARBS	**599 CALS**

Weight: 370g

Dauphinoise Potatoes

10g CARBS   **178 CALS**

Weight: 72g

20g CARBS   **363 CALS**

Weight: 147g

30g CARBS   **548 CALS**

Weight: 222g

40g CARBS   **734 CALS**

Weight: 297g

50g CARBS   **921 CALS**

Weight: 373g

60g CARBS   **1107 CALS**

Weight: 448g

Gnocchi

30g CARBS **136 CALS**

Weight: 80g

60g CARBS **272 CALS**

Weight: 160g

90g CARBS **408 CALS**

Weight: 240g

120g CARBS **547 CALS**

Weight: 322g

150g CARBS **683 CALS**

Weight: 402g

180g CARBS **819 CALS**

Weight: 482g

Jacket Potato (with skin)

20g CARBS   **95 CALS**

Weight: 95g

35g CARBS   **160 CALS**

Weight: 158g

45g CARBS   **211 CALS**

Weight: 220g

60g CARBS   **280 CALS**

Weight: 284g

75g CARBS   **351 CALS**

Weight: 348g

90g CARBS   **407 CALS**

Weight: 410g

Mashed Potato

20g CARBS	86 CALS

Weight: 120g

40g CARBS	169 CALS

Weight: 235g

60g CARBS	256 CALS

Weight: 355g

80g CARBS	338 CALS

Weight: 470g

100g CARBS	425 CALS

Weight: 590g

120g CARBS	508 CALS

Weight: 705g

New Potatoes

10g CARBS   **43 CALS**

Weight: 65g

20g CARBS   **86 CALS**

Weight: 130g

30g CARBS   **129 CALS**

Weight: 195g

40g CARBS   **172 CALS**

Weight: 260g

60g CARBS   **257 CALS**

Weight: 390g

80g CARBS   **343 CALS**

Weight: 520g

Potato Faces

10g CARBS   **65 CALS**

Weight: 34g

20g CARBS   **131 CALS**

Weight: 68g

30g CARBS   **196 CALS**

Weight: 102g

40g CARBS   **261 CALS**

Weight: 136g

50g CARBS   **326 CALS**

Weight: 170g

60g CARBS   **392 CALS**

Weight: 204g

Roast Potatoes

10g CARBS   **57 CALS**

Weight: 38g

25g CARBS   **142 CALS**

Weight: 95g

40g CARBS   **231 CALS**

Weight: 155g

55g CARBS   **316 CALS**

Weight: 212g

70g CARBS   **402 CALS**

Weight: 270g

85g CARBS   **492 CALS**

Weight: 330g

Sauté Potatoes (baked)

10g CARBS	62 CALS

Weight: 28g

20g CARBS	121 CALS

Weight: 55g

30g CARBS	176 CALS

Weight: 80g

40g CARBS	238 CALS

Weight: 108g

50g CARBS	297 CALS

Weight: 135g

60g CARBS	356 CALS

Weight: 162g

Sweet Potatoes (baked)

15g CARBS   **63 CALS**

Weight: 55g

30g CARBS   **124 CALS**

Weight: 108g

45g CARBS   **184 CALS**

Weight: 160g

60g CARBS   **247 CALS**

Weight: 215g

75g CARBS   **311 CALS**

Weight: 270g

90g CARBS   **370 CALS**

Weight: 322g

Wedges

10g CARBS **68 CALS**

Weight: 55g

20g CARBS **135 CALS**

Weight: 110g

30g CARBS **203 CALS**

Weight: 165g

40g CARBS **271 CALS**

Weight: 220g

50g CARBS **332 CALS**

Weight: 270g

60g CARBS **400 CALS**

Weight: 325g

Hash Brown

10g CARBS | **88 CALS**

	CARBS	CALS
2x	20g	176
3x	30g	264
4x	40g	352
Weight: 44g		

Potato Croquette

5g CARBS | **47 CALS**

	CARBS	CALS
2x	10g	94
3x	15g	141
4x	20g	188
Weight: 22g		

Potato Rosti

20g CARBS | **155 CALS**

	CARBS	CALS
2x	40g	310
3x	60g	465
4x	80g	620
Weight: 80g		

Potato Waffle

15g CARBS | **98 CALS**

	CARBS	CALS
2x	30g	196
3x	45g	294
4x	60g	392
Weight: 49g		

Bulgar Wheat

20g CARBS	94 CALS

Weight: 100g

40g CARBS	188 CALS

Weight: 200g

60g CARBS	277 CALS

Weight: 295g

Quinoa

20g CARBS	109 CALS

Weight: 85g

40g CARBS	220 CALS

Weight: 172g

60g CARBS	333 CALS

Weight: 260g

Couscous

10g CARBS   **50 CALS**

Weight: 45g

25g CARBS   **121 CALS**

Weight: 110g

40g CARBS   **193 CALS**

Weight: 175g

55g CARBS   **264 CALS**

Weight: 240g

70g CARBS   **336 CALS**

Weight: 305g

85g CARBS   **407 CALS**

Weight: 370g

Noodles (egg)

20g CARBS   **101 CALS**

Weight: 58g

40g CARBS   **200 CALS**

Weight: 115g

60g CARBS   **296 CALS**

Weight: 170g

80g CARBS   **397 CALS**

Weight: 228g

100g CARBS   **496 CALS**

Weight: 285g

120g CARBS   **595 CALS**

Weight: 342g

Noodles (rice)

20g CARBS | **86 CALS**

Weight: 70g

40g CARBS | **175 CALS**

Weight: 142g

60g CARBS | **264 CALS**

Weight: 215g

80g CARBS | **351 CALS**

Weight: 285g

100g CARBS | **440 CALS**

Weight: 358g

120g CARBS | **529 CALS**

Weight: 430g

Pasta (bows)

10g CARBS	**50 CALS**

Weight: 30g

30g CARBS	**148 CALS**

Weight: 88g

50g CARBS	**249 CALS**

Weight: 148g

70g CARBS	**344 CALS**

Weight: 205g

90g CARBS	**445 CALS**

Weight: 265g

110g CARBS	**543 CALS**

Weight: 323g

Pasta (macaroni)

10g CARBS | **49 CALS**

Weight: 32g

30g CARBS | **152 CALS**

Weight: 100g

50g CARBS | **252 CALS**

Weight: 166g

70g CARBS | **354 CALS**

Weight: 233g

90g CARBS | **456 CALS**

Weight: 300g

110g CARBS | **556 CALS**

Weight: 366g

Pasta (penne)

10g CARBS   **50 CALS**

Weight: 30g

30g CARBS   **150 CALS**

Weight: 90g

50g CARBS   **247 CALS**

Weight: 148g

70g CARBS   **347 CALS**

Weight: 208g

90g CARBS   **443 CALS**

Weight: 265g

110g CARBS   **543 CALS**

Weight: 325g

Pasta (shells)

10g CARBS   **50 CALS**

Weight: 30g

30g CARBS   **147 CALS**

Weight: 88g

50g CARBS   **247 CALS**

Weight: 148g

70g CARBS   **342 CALS**

Weight: 205g

90g CARBS   **443 CALS**

Weight: 265g

110g CARBS   **539 CALS**

Weight: 323g

Pasta (tagliatelle)

10g CARBS   **53 CALS**

Weight: 30g

30g CARBS   **158 CALS**

Weight: 90g

50g CARBS   **263 CALS**

Weight: 150g

70g CARBS   **368 CALS**

Weight: 210g

90g CARBS   **473 CALS**

Weight: 270g

110g CARBS   **578 CALS**

Weight: 330g

Pasta (twirls)

10g CARBS   **50 CALS**

Weight: 30g

30g CARBS   **148 CALS**

Weight: 88g

50g CARBS   **249 CALS**

Weight: 148g

70g CARBS   **344 CALS**

Weight: 205g

90g CARBS   **445 CALS**

Weight: 265g

110g CARBS   **543 CALS**

Weight: 323g

Pasta (twists)

10g CARBS   **51 CALS**

Weight: 30g

30g CARBS   **149 CALS**

Weight: 88g

50g CARBS   **245 CALS**

Weight: 145g

70g CARBS   **343 CALS**

Weight: 203g

90g CARBS   **439 CALS**

Weight: 260g

110g CARBS   **537 CALS**

Weight: 318g

Pasta (vermicelli)

10g CARBS   **52 CALS**

Weight: 40g

30g CARBS   **161 CALS**

Weight: 125g

50g CARBS   **271 CALS**

Weight: 210g

70g CARBS   **374 CALS**

Weight: 290g

90g CARBS   **484 CALS**

Weight: 375g

110g CARBS   **593 CALS**

Weight: 460g

Rice (white)

10g CARBS	44 CALS

Weight: 32g

30g CARBS	132 CALS

Weight: 96g

50g CARBS	225 CALS

Weight: 163g

70g CARBS	311 CALS

Weight: 225g

90g CARBS	400 CALS

Weight: 290g

110g CARBS	490 CALS

Weight: 355g

Rice (brown)

10g CARBS   **42 CALS**

Weight: 30g

30g CARBS   **134 CALS**

Weight: 95g

50g CARBS   **219 CALS**

Weight: 155g

70g CARBS   **307 CALS**

Weight: 218g

90g CARBS   **395 CALS**

Weight: 280g

110g CARBS   **484 CALS**

Weight: 343g

Rice (sticky white)

20g CARBS	104 CALS

Weight: 80g

40g CARBS	202 CALS

Weight: 155g

60g CARBS	306 CALS

Weight: 235g

Polenta

10g CARBS	47 CALS

Weight: 65g

20g CARBS	93 CALS

Weight: 130g

30g CARBS	137 CALS

Weight: 190g

Ravioli (fresh, meat-filled)

10g CARBS   **70 CALS**

Weight: 40g

30g CARBS   **200 CALS**

Weight: 115g

50g CARBS   **334 CALS**

Weight: 192g

70g CARBS   **470 CALS**

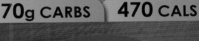

Weight: 270g

90g CARBS   **600 CALS**

Weight: 345g

110g CARBS   **734 CALS**

Weight: 422g

Spaghetti (white)

10g CARBS **52 CALS**

Weight: 33g

30g CARBS **149 CALS**

Weight: 95g

50g CARBS **248 CALS**

Weight: 158g

70g CARBS **345 CALS**

Weight: 220g

90g CARBS **447 CALS**

Weight: 285g

110g CARBS **546 CALS**

Weight: 348g

Spaghetti (wholemeal)

10g CARBS **48 CALS**

Weight: 33g

30g CARBS **151 CALS**

Weight: 105g

50g CARBS **248 CALS**

Weight: 172g

70g CARBS **346 CALS**

Weight: 240g

90g CARBS **446 CALS**

Weight: 310g

110g CARBS **547 CALS**

Weight: 380g

Tortellini (fresh, cheese-filled)

15g CARBS   **103 CALS**

Weight: 42g

50g CARBS   **348 CALS**

Weight: 142g

85g CARBS   **593 CALS**

Weight: 242g

120g CARBS   **838 CALS**

Weight: 342g

155g CARBS   **1083 CALS**

Weight: 442g

190g CARBS   **1328 CALS**

Weight: 542g

Pasta Shapes (tinned)

8g CARBS   **41 CALS**

Weight: 70g

17g CARBS   **81 CALS**

Weight: 140g

25g CARBS   **122 CALS**

Weight: 210g (half tin)

34g CARBS   **165 CALS**

Weight: 285g

43g CARBS   **206 CALS**

Weight: 355g

51g CARBS   **247 CALS**

Weight: 425g (full tin)

Ravioli in Tomato Sauce (tinned)

7g CARBS   **49 CALS**

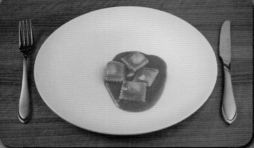

Weight: 70g

14g CARBS   **98 CALS**

Weight: 140g

22g CARBS   **147 CALS**

Weight: 210g (half tin)

29g CARBS   **200 CALS**

Weight: 285g

37g CARBS   **249 CALS**

Weight: 355g

44g CARBS   **298 CALS**

Weight: 425g (full tin)

Spaghetti in Tomato Sauce (tinned)

10g CARBS   **45 CALS**

Weight: 70g

20g CARBS   **90 CALS**

Weight: 140g

30g CARBS   **134 CALS**

Weight: 210g (half tin)

40g CARBS   **182 CALS**

Weight: 285g

50g CARBS   **227 CALS**

Weight: 355g

60g CARBS   **272 CALS**

Weight: 425g (full tin)

Spaghetti Hoops in Tomato Sauce (tinned)

9g CARBS	42 CALS

Weight: 70g

18g CARBS	84 CALS

Weight: 140g

28g CARBS	126 CALS

Weight: 210g (half tin)

37g CARBS	168 CALS

Weight: 280g

46g CARBS	210 CALS

Weight: 350g

55g CARBS	252 CALS

Weight: 420g (full tin)

Crisps

10g CARBS   **95 CALS**

Weight: 18g

20g CARBS   **201 CALS**

Weight: 38g

30g CARBS   **297 CALS**

Weight: 56g

40g CARBS   **398 CALS**

Weight: 75g

50g CARBS   **498 CALS**

Weight: 94g

60g CARBS   **594 CALS**

Weight: 112g

Bombay Mix

10g CARBS · **141** CALS

Weight: 28g

20g CARBS · **282** CALS

Weight: 56g

30g CARBS · **428** CALS

Weight: 85g

Cashew Nuts

5g CARBS · **171** CALS

Weight: 28g

10g CARBS · **336** CALS

Weight: 55g

15g CARBS · **489** CALS

Weight: 80g

Dried Fruit & Nuts

10g CARBS   **92 CALS**

Weight: 22g

20g CARBS   **185 CALS**

Weight: 44g

30g CARBS   **277 CALS**

Weight: 66g

Peanuts (roasted)

5g CARBS   **421 CALS**

Weight: 70g

10g CARBS   **843 CALS**

Weight: 140g

15g CARBS   **1264 CALS**

Weight: 210g

Popcorn (plain)

5g CARBS	59 CALS

Weight: 10g

10g CARBS	118 CALS

Weight: 20g

15g CARBS	178 CALS

Weight: 30g

20g CARBS	243 CALS

Weight: 41g

25g CARBS	302 CALS

Weight: 51g

30g CARBS	361 CALS

Weight: 61g

Popcorn (sweet)

20g CARBS **92 CALS**

Weight: 22g

40g CARBS **187 CALS**

Weight: 45g

60g CARBS **283 CALS**

Weight: 68g

80g CARBS **374 CALS**

Weight: 90g

100g CARBS **470 CALS**

Weight: 113g

120g CARBS **562 CALS**

Weight: 135g

Prawn Crackers

5g CARBS **51 CALS**

Weight: 9g

10g CARBS **103 CALS**

Weight: 18g

20g CARBS **200 CALS**

Weight: 35g

30g CARBS **296 CALS**

Weight: 52g

40g CARBS **388 CALS**

Weight: 68g

50g CARBS **490 CALS**

Weight: 86g

Tortilla Chips

10g CARBS | **30 CALS**

Weight: 16g

30g CARBS | **230 CALS**

Weight: 50g

60g CARBS | **459 CALS**

Weight: 100g

Houmous

5g CARBS | **84 CALS**

Weight: 45g

10g CARBS | **168 CALS**

Weight: 90g

15g CARBS | **243 CALS**

Weight: 130g

Pretzels

10g CARBS   **49 CALS**

Weight: 13g

20g CARBS   **99 CALS**

Weight: 26g

30g CARBS   **152 CALS**

Weight: 40g

Fudge

10g CARBS   **53 CALS**

Weight: 12g

20g CARBS   **110 CALS**

Weight: 25g

30g CARBS   **162 CALS**

Weight: 37g

Chocolate (milk)

10g CARBS   **85 CALS**

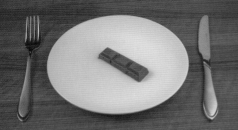

Weight: 16g

20g CARBS   **175 CALS**

Weight: 33g

30g CARBS   **265 CALS**

Weight: 50g

40g CARBS   **354 CALS**

Weight: 67g

50g CARBS   **450 CALS**

Weight: 85g

60g CARBS   **534 CALS**

Weight: 101g

Chocolate (dark)

10g CARBS **82** CALS  Weight: 16g	**20g** CARBS **163** CALS  Weight: 32g
30g CARBS **245** CALS  Weight: 48g	**40g** CARBS **321** CALS  Weight: 63g
50g CARBS **398** CALS  Weight: 78g	**60g** CARBS **479** CALS  Weight: 94g

Chocolate Mint

10g CARBS	75 CALS

	CARBS	CALS
2x	20g	150
3x	30g	225
4x	40g	300
Weight: 15g		

Licorice Allsorts

10g CARBS	43 CALS

	CARBS	CALS
2x	20g	86
3x	30g	129
4x	40g	172
Weight: 12g		

Individual Chocolate

7g CARBS	52 CALS

	CARBS	CALS
2x	14g	104
3x	21g	156
4x	28g	208
Weight: 11g		

8g CARBS	76 CALS

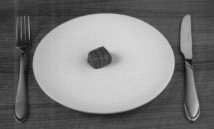

	CARBS	CALS
2x	16g	152
3x	24g	228
4x	32g	304
Weight: 14g		

Cola Bottles

10g CARBS	46 CALS

	CARBS	CALS
2x	20g	92
3x	30g	138
4x	40g	184
Weight: 13g		

Jelly Babies

12g CARBS	60 CALS

	CARBS	CALS
2x	24g	120
3x	36g	180
4x	48g	240
Weight: 18g		

Jelly Beans

10g CARBS	42 CALS

	CARBS	CALS
2x	20g	84
3x	30g	126
4x	40g	168
Weight: 11g		

Wine Gums

10g CARBS	41 CALS

	CARBS	CALS
2x	20g	82
3x	30g	123
4x	40g	164
Weight: 14g		

Fish Stew with Jollof Rice

40g CARBS   **388 CALS**

Weight: 275g

85g CARBS   **811 CALS**

Weight: 575g

125g CARBS   **1199 CALS**

Weight: 850g

Fufu

35g CARBS   **140 CALS**

Weight: 130g

70g CARBS   **286 CALS**

Weight: 265g

100g CARBS   **405 CALS**

Weight: 375g

Beef Burger

30g CARBS   **532** CALS

Weight: 200g

French Fries

30g CARBS   **269** CALS

Weight: 96g (small)

Chicken Burger

45g CARBS   **398** CALS

Weight: 168g

50g CARBS   **448** CALS

Weight: 160g (medium)

Veggie Burger

35g CARBS   **340** CALS

Weight: 158g

70g CARBS   **636** CALS

Weight: 227g (large)

Caribbean - Fried Fish, Rice & Peas

60g CARBS | **470 CALS**

Weight: 265g

115g CARBS | **940 CALS**

Weight: 530g

Caribbean - Goat Curry, Rice & Peas

55g CARBS | **630 CALS**

Weight: 375g

110g CARBS | **1260 CALS**

Weight: 750g

Caribbean - Jerk Chicken, Rice & Peas

55g CARBS | **600 CALS**

Weight: 405g

110g CARBS | **1200 CALS**

Weight: 810g

Caribbean - Jamaican Beef Patty

20g CARBS	206 CALS

Weight: 85g

40g CARBS	407 CALS

Weight: 170g

Caribbean - Rice & Peas

50g CARBS	263 CALS

Weight: 150g (half tray)

100g CARBS	525 CALS

Weight: 300g (full tray)

Chinese - Duck Pancake

5g CARBS	95 CALS

Weight: 50g

5g CARBS	95 CALS

Weight: 50g

Chinese - Chicken Balls

7g CARBS   **74 CALS**

Weight: 38g

28g CARBS   **272 CALS**

Weight: 140g (half tray)

55g CARBS   **543 CALS**

Weight: 280g (full tray)

Chinese - Prawn Toast

5g CARBS   **123 CALS**

Weight: 32g

10g CARBS   **234 CALS**

Weight: 61g

15g CARBS   **345 CALS**

Weight: 90g (full tray)

Chinese - Beef Chow Mein

| 40g CARBS | 374 CALS | 80g CARBS | 741 CALS |

Weight: 275g (half tray)

Weight: 545g (full tray)

Chinese - Chicken Curry

| 5g CARBS | 276 CALS | 10g CARBS | 551 CALS |

Weight: 190g (half tray)

Weight: 380g (full tray)

Chinese - Singapore Noodles

| 25g CARBS | 338 CALS | 50g CARBS | 677 CALS |

Weight: 205g (half tray)

Weight: 410g (full tray)

Chinese - Egg Fried Rice

60g CARBS	335 CALS

Weight: 180g (half tray)

120g CARBS	670 CALS

Weight: 360g (full tray)

Chinese - Spring Roll

5g CARBS	52 CALS

Weight: 24g

15g CARBS	152 CALS

Weight: 70g

Chinese - Spare Ribs

20g CARBS	405 CALS

Weight: 150g (half tray)

40g CARBS	824 CALS

Weight: 305g (full tray)

Chip Shop - Fish

10g CARBS	269 CALS

Weight: 135g

Chip Shop - Chips

40g CARBS	311 CALS

Weight: 130g

25g CARBS	657 CALS

Weight: 330g

80g CARBS	626 CALS

Weight: 262g

Battered Sausage

30g CARBS	410 CALS

Weight: 137g

120g CARBS	944 CALS

Weight: 395g

Indian - Onion Bhaji

10g CARBS | **195 CALS**

Weight: 66g

10g CARBS | **195 CALS**

Weight: 66g

Indian - Pakora

5g CARBS | **52 CALS**

Weight: 22g

10g CARBS | **106 CALS**

Weight: 45g

Indian - Samosa (meat)

5g CARBS | **178 CALS**

Weight: 30g

10g CARBS | **344 CALS**

Weight: 58g

Indian - Chicken Tikka Masala

5g CARBS   **290** CALS

10g CARBS   **581** CALS

Weight: 185g (half tray)

Weight: 370g (full tray)

Indian - King Prawn Bhuna

5g CARBS   **133** CALS

10g CARBS   **266** CALS

Weight: 175g (half tray)

Weight: 350g (full tray)

Indian - Lamb Rogan Josh

10g CARBS   **306** CALS

20g CARBS   **613** CALS

Weight: 175g (half tray)

Weight: 350g (full tray)

Indian - Bombay Potatoes

15g CARBS   **164 CALS**

Weight: 150g (half tray)

30g CARBS   **327 CALS**

Weight: 300g (full tray)

Indian - Sag Aloo Gobi

10g CARBS   **164 CALS**

Weight: 130g (half tray)

20g CARBS   **328 CALS**

Weight: 260g (full tray)

Indian - Sweet Mango Chutney

10g CARBS   **39 CALS**

Weight: 16g

20g CARBS   **80 CALS**

Weight: 33g

Doner Kebab (small)
50g CARBS   **584** CALS

Weight: 250g

Doner Kebab (large)
80g CARBS   **1053** CALS

Weight: 415g

Shish Kebab (small)
50g CARBS   **439** CALS

Weight: 250g

Shish Kebab (large)
80g CARBS   **762** CALS

Weight: 415g

Falafel in Pitta (small)
60g CARBS   **363** CALS

Weight: 200g

Falafel in Pitta (large)
100g CARBS   **647** CALS

Weight: 350g

Pizza (deep pan)

20g CARBS — 182 CALS

	CARBS	CALS
2x	40g	364
3x	60g	546
4x	80g	728
Weight: 70g		

40g CARBS — 364 CALS

	CARBS	CALS
2x	80g	728
3x	120g	1092
4x	160g	1456
Weight: 140g		

60g CARBS — 541 CALS

	CARBS	CALS
2x	120g	1082
3x	180g	1623
4x	240g	2164
Weight: 208g		

80g CARBS — 720 CALS

	CARBS	CALS
2x	160g	1440
3x	240g	2160
4x	320g	2880
Weight: 277g		

Pizza (thin crust)

10g CARBS　108 CALS

	CARBS	CALS
2x	20g	216
3x	30g	324
4x	40g	432
Weight: 50g		

20g CARBS　216 CALS

	CARBS	CALS
2x	40g	432
3x	60g	648
4x	80g	864
Weight: 100g		

30g CARBS　324 CALS

	CARBS	CALS
2x	60g	648
3x	90g	972
4x	120g	1296
Weight: 150g		

40g CARBS　432 CALS

	CARBS	CALS
2x	80g	864
3x	120g	1296
4x	160g	1728
Weight: 200g		

Pizza (stuffed crust)

20g CARBS   153 CALS

	CARBS	CALS
2x	40g	306
3x	60g	459
4x	80g	612
Weight: 65g		

40g CARBS   306 CALS

	CARBS	CALS
2x	80g	612
3x	120g	918
4x	160g	1224
Weight: 130g		

60g CARBS   465 CALS

	CARBS	CALS
2x	120g	930
3x	180g	1395
4x	240g	1860
Weight: 198g		

80g CARBS   616 CALS

	CARBS	CALS
2x	160g	1232
3x	240g	1848
4x	320g	2464
Weight: 262g		

Thai - Green Curry

10g CARBS	197 CALS

Weight: 195g (half tray)

20g CARBS	394 CALS

Weight: 390g (full tray)

Thai - Phad Thai

35g CARBS	252 CALS

Weight: 200g (half tray)

70g CARBS	504 CALS

Weight: 400g (full tray)

Thai - Pineapple, Chicken & Prawn Rice

75g CARBS	550 CALS

Weight: 250g (half tray)

150g CARBS	1100 CALS

Weight: 500g (full tray)

Baked Beans in Tomato Sauce

10g CARBS	55 CALS

Weight: 65g

20g CARBS	109 CALS

Weight: 130g

30g CARBS	164 CALS

Weight: 195g (half tin)

40g CARBS	218 CALS

Weight: 260g

50g CARBS	273 CALS

Weight: 325g

60g CARBS	328 CALS

Weight: 390g (full tin)

Chick Peas

5g CARBS | **35** CALS

Weight: 30g

10g CARBS | **69** CALS

Weight: 60g

20g CARBS | **144** CALS

Weight: 125g

Lentils

10g CARBS | **63** CALS

Weight: 60g

20g CARBS | **126** CALS

Weight: 120g

30g CARBS | **189** CALS

Weight: 180g

Kidney Beans

5g CARBS   **30 CALS**

Weight: 30g

Mung Beans

5g CARBS   **27 CALS**

Weight: 30g

10g CARBS   **55 CALS**

Weight: 55g

10g CARBS   **59 CALS**

Weight: 65g

20g CARBS   **115 CALS**

Weight: 115g

15g CARBS   **86 CALS**

Weight: 95g

Peas

5g CARBS | **35 CALS**

Weight: 50g

10g CARBS | **69 CALS**

Weight: 100g

15g CARBS | **104 CALS**

Weight: 150g

Mushy Peas

10g CARBS | **61 CALS**

Weight: 75g

20g CARBS | **117 CALS**

Weight: 145g

40g CARBS | **243 CALS**

Weight: 300g

Parsnips

10g CARBS　**82** CALS

Weight: 60g

20g CARBS　**156** CALS

Weight: 115g

30g CARBS　**238** CALS

Weight: 175g

Butternut Squash

10g CARBS　**42** CALS

Weight: 130g

20g CARBS　**85** CALS

Weight: 265g

30g CARBS　**128** CALS

Weight: 400g

Sweetcorn

10g CARBS	46 CALS

Weight: 38g

20g CARBS	92 CALS

Weight: 75g

40g CARBS	183 CALS

Weight: 150g

Corn on the Cob

5g CARBS	29 CALS

Weight: 44g

10g CARBS	56 CALS

Weight: 85g

20g CARBS	112 CALS

Weight: 170g

Plantain (fried)

20g CARBS **112 CALS**

Weight: 42g

40g CARBS **224 CALS**

Weight: 84g

60g CARBS **336 CALS**

Weight: 126g

Yam (boiled)

20g CARBS **80 CALS**

Weight: 60g

40g CARBS **160 CALS**

Weight: 120g

60g CARBS **242 CALS**

Weight: 182g

Index

Acknowledgements

We hope that you have enjoyed this book and continue to find it useful for years to come. The book was made from a fantastic idea between two great friends, and turned into the reality that you see before you. It has been great fun producing the final product and we hope it helps thousands of people to understand the carbohydrate and calorie content of the food they eat.

We would like to take the opportunity to express our deepest thanks and appreciation to the two most special people in our lives - Justine and Chrissi. They have managed to put up with us over the last year during the production of the book. Not only have they helped in the shopping, making and weighing of food, they have also been subjected to our endless conversations about the book, multiple photo shoots and consumption of a large number of cakes, snacks and other food to ensure it didn't go to waste. A big thanks also to Justine for allowing us the use of the flat for all the photo shoots and the loss of the dining table for over 3 months!

We would also like to thank the following people for their advice, support and kind words:

- The Diabetes Management and Education Group (DMEG) committee of the British Dietetic Association
- Reviewers of the book: Anita Beckwith, Emma Jenkins, Victoria Deprez, Marianne Ouaknin, Jasmine Walton
- Centremark Design
- Ravinder Kundi
- Friends and Family
- Peter Rose
- Barry and Joan Cheyette
- Pat & Akbar Balolia

Data Sources

Nutritional information in this book was gathered using a variety of sources. Where available, carbohydrate and calorie values were taken from McCance and Widdowson's *The Composition of Foods*. Other reference values were taken using an average from commercially available products.

Please note that values in this book are to be used as a guide only. The authors cannot accept any liability for any consequences arising from the use of the information contained within this book. Every effort has been made to ensure figures represent a true and fair value of carbohydrate and calorie content of food & drinks included, but these values can vary between brands and food preparation methods.

About the Authors

Chris Cheyette MSc BSc (Hons) RD
Diabetes Specialist Dietitian

Chris qualified as a dietitian in 2000, and has been working full-time for the NHS ever since. Since 2003, he has been a Diabetes Specialist Dietitian, working with a wide range of people with Type 1, Type 2 and gestational diabetes.

Chris has worked on a number of projects over the years, many with a goal of improving the educational resources that are currently on offer to people with diabetes. These include an educational DVD for young people with diabetes, which earned him the 2007 British Dietetic Association Elizabeth Washington Award and a short-listing for the 2006 Diabetes UK Education Award.

Chris has also published a number of journal articles relating to diabetes and weight management. He regularly undertakes local and national presentations to health professionals in the field of diabetes and has done a number of television and newspaper interviews.

As well as his NHS duties, Chris is an elected member of the UK Advisory council for Diabetes UK. He is also a committee member of the Diabetes Management & Education Group of the British Dietetic Association.

Yello Balolia BA (Hons)
Photographic Artist

In August 2003 Canada-born, Blackpool-bred Yello bought his first ever camera. He soon proceeded to give up his full-time job as a TV Dubbing Mixer and turn to a visual-based career.

Having since achieved a 1st Class Honours Degree in Photography, Yello has undertaken a series of creative projects including private photographic commissions (www.yellobalolia.com).

Thriving to achieve the best image quality possible, Yello still primarily uses traditional film cameras for his photographic art projects. He captures, manipulates and prints all the images himself in order to ensure that the end product is second to none.

Carbs & Cals provides a quick, visual guide to the amount of carbohydrate and calories in a wide selection of food and drinks. With over 1,200 photos, it is a fast reference for carb counting, calorie counting and choosing the most appropriate portion size.

Whether you are a person with diabetes, someone trying to lose weight, or a healthcare professional, this book is for you.

Carbs & Cals was compiled by
Chris Cheyette MSc BSc (Hons) RD, Diabetes Specialist Dietitian
& Yello Balolia BA (Hons), Photographic Artist

Fish (battered)

20g CARBS | **218 CALS**

Weight: 130g

40g CARBS | **445 CALS**

Weight: 265g

Chips (oven)

30g CARBS | **162 CALS**

Weight: 100g

90g CARBS | **491 CALS**

Weight: 303g

£12.99

Chello Publishing Limited

ISBN 978-0-9564430-1-4

© **Mixed Sources**
Product group from well-managed forests, controlled sources and recycled wood or fiber
www.fsc.org   Cert no. SGS-COC-0040
© 1996 Forest Stewardship Council

FSC

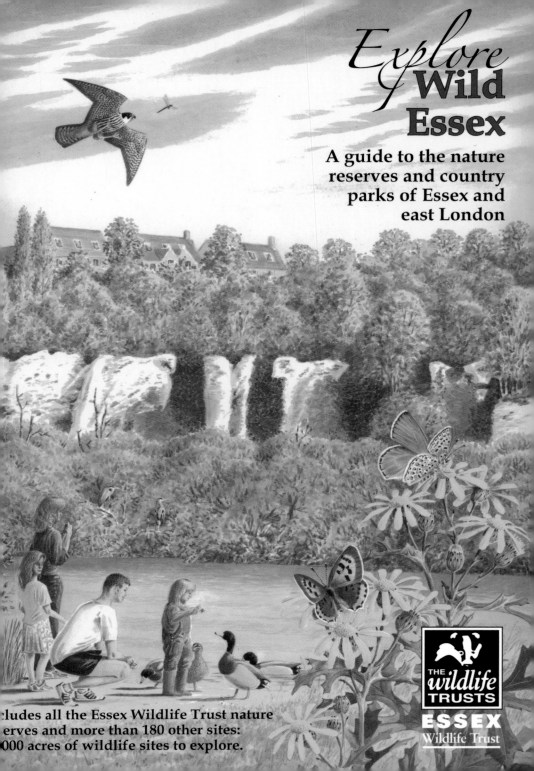

Explore Wild Essex

A guide to the nature reserves and country parks of Essex and east London

:ludes all the Essex Wildlife Trust nature
erves and more than 180 other sites:
000 acres of wildlife sites to explore.

THE **wildlife** TRUSTS

ESSEX
Wildlife Trust